1995

THE BEST OF QUINTANA

THE BEST OF
QUINTANA

by
PATRICIA QUINTANA
photographs by IGNACIO URQUIZA
and JORGE CONTRERAS CHACEL

Stewart, Tabori & Chang

Published and distributed in the U.S. by Stewart, Tabori and Chang, 575 Broadway, New York,
New York 10012. Distributed in Canada by General Publishing, 30 Lesmill Road, Don Mills,
Ontario M3B 2T6. Distributed in the U.K. by Hi Marketing, 38 Carver Road, London SE24 9LT.
Distributed in Europe by Onslow Books Limited, Tyler's Court, 111A Wardour Street,
London W1V 3 TD. Distributed in Australia and New Zealand by Peribo Pty Limited,
58 Beamont Road, Mount Kuing Gai NSW 2080.

Edited by BRENDA GOLDBERG and MARY KALAMARAS
Designed by NAI Y. CHANG
Production by ALICE WONG and CHRISTOPHER YOUNG
Photo Credits:
IGNACIO URQUIZA: 2-3, 4-5, 6, 7, 8-9 (all), 12-13 (all), 14-15, 17 (all), 18, 19, 20, 22, 24-25, 26, 28-
29, 31, 32-33, 34, 36, 39, 40, 42, 43 (both), 46-47, 48-49, 50, 51, 56-57, 58, 62-63, 64, 65, 67,
70-71, 73, 83, 90-91, 99, 101, 102-03, 110-111, 112, 116-117, 121, 122-123, 128.
JORGE CONTRERAS CHACEL: 53, 55, 69, 77, 78, 81, 86-87, 93, 95, 97, 100, 104, 107, 109, 124.

Library of Congress Cataloging-in-Publication Data
Quintana, Patricia.
        The best of Quintana / by Patricia Quintana : photographs by
Ignacio Urquiza and Jorge Contreras Chacel.
        p.   cm.
        Includes index.
        ISBN 1-55670-409-7   : $22.50 ($31.50 Can.)
        1. Cookery, Mexican.   I. Title.
TX716. M4Q54   1995
641.5972—dc20   94-45985
                                                           CIP

FRONT COVER: Empanadas al Achiote Rellenas de Camarón, recipe on page 30.
BACK COVER: Mangoes.
PAGES 2-3: Silhouette of colonial church at dusk.
PAGES 4-5: The Cañamelar coffee plantation makes a dramatic setting for this house.
PAGE 6: Apples being sold at market.
PAGE 7: Mamey fruits, called *zapote*, in Tabasco.
PAGES 8-9: Left: Sinaloan sea bass, fresh from the market.
Center: Fresh pomegranate seeds are puréed with water and sugar for a refreshing drink.
Right: Calla lilies are abundant in San Miguel de Allende.

FOREWORD

Prólogo

For more than twenty years, my greatest passion has been cooking. I have spent much of my time studying and researching the secrets of Mexican gastronomy, as well as the culinary roots of many other places in the world. With time and experience, I have developed a particular cuisine based on the different ancient cultures of my country—Maya, Zapotec, Totonac, Toltec, and Aztec. Each of these cultures has a distinctive culinary tradition that is both rich and diverse.

In each of my gastronomic tours across the Mexican Republic, I have discovered a vast culinary mosaic. Each province has developed its own singular cuisine but there is a similarity in the use of regional products. Thus, Mexican cuisine becomes the bond that joins all of the states and identifies them as native sons of this wonderful land.

Over the years, my gastronomic repertoire has grown, enriched by a culinary fusion with cooking traditions of other continents. Today, my work celebrates many different tastes and techniques: the simplicity of *tortillas*, the complexity of *mole poblano*, the freshness of *jícama and orange salad*, the temptation of *chiles en nogada*, as well as a hearty *pozole* or the distinctive taste of a *beef filet with morels in a chile-cream sauce*.

Aside from my traveling and learning experiences, the publication of my cook books has been one of my greatest satisfactions. Writing these books has enriched my life and helped me to grow professionally.

Over the years, I have selected my favorite recipes and they are gathered together in this book. These sixty recipes have become staples for me and for the many people with whom I work. This book represents both my personal favorites and theirs. These are my most cherished dishes because they have been prepared for special occasions such as birthdays, baptisms, and weddings. Sometimes, however, the dish itself is so special that it makes the occasion an unforgettable memory and these recipes have also been included in this book.

The Best of Quintana is the tenth book I have published and it is very special to me as it represents my feelings, my tastes, my preferences, and my own way of understanding and cooking Mexican dishes.

It is also my invitation to you to share with me the recipes that are trademarks of both my personal work and the profound culinary customs of my country.

PATRICIA QUINTANA
DECEMBER, 1994

CONTENTS

LA TORTILLA ◆ TORTILLAS

The tortilla, the Mexican food for which there are no frontiers, is our plate, our spoon. It might enfold any number of ingredients, from a sauce to a few grains of salt, a slice of meat to a serving of stew, a piece of fowl or fish to some beans, some mash to a slice of cheese. The tortilla cannot be absent from the daily table. The dough is cooked on a clay *comal* (a skillet) cured with lime or on one made with a thin metal sheet. The dough has its secrets. It has to be kneaded with salt and water until it is soft, pliable, and moist enough to be flattened between the palms of the hands or with the aid of fragrant leaves, such as those of the banana tree. Today, the tortillas can be pressed by putting a ball of dough between plastic sheets, with the size of the tortilla determined by the amount used.

Tortillas can be small and thin or large and thick or even huge, like the *tayudas* of Oaxaca. They can be soft like those sold in narrow-mouthed palm baskets wrapped in embroidered cloths to keep them warm. Sometimes tortillas are dyed with natural colors—green, pink, or purple—or flavored with different chiles, such as *ancho, pasilla, cascabel,* or *guajillo*. The tortilla has formed part of the daily eating ritual since Quetzalcoatl went up the hill of food, was transformed into an ant, and deposited the sacred grain, which has become the base of the tortilla. They are eaten soft, toasted, hard, or fried, and lend themselves to various uses, such as in *tacos, tostadas*, and *chilaquiles*.

2 1/4 pounds fresh white, blue, yellow, or purple
    cornmeal
1/3 to 1/2 cup water
1/4 teaspoon salt

Prepare the dough: Preheat the *comal* for 20 minutes. Prepare the tortillas with a metal or wooden tortilla press with 2 squares of plastic the size of the machine. Spread the dough on a clean work-surface and sprinkle it with a bit of water and salt. Knead it until it is smooth and soft. Add a little more water and continue kneading until the dough is moist but not sticky. Cover it with a damp cloth and let it rest for 15 minutes. Before making the tortillas, knead the dough again and form balls 1 1/2 to 2 1/2 inches in diameter. Open the tortilla machine and line the base with a sheet of plastic. Place the ball of dough in the middle, cover the ball with the other sheet of plastic, and press it, not so much that it sticks. Turn it over and press lightly until it is even. Take off the plastic frame and with the palm of the hand hit the tortilla with a twisting motion. (This will make it rise during cooking.) With moist hands, carefully peel the tortilla from the other plastic frame and let it slide from your hand to the comal. Cook for a few minutes before flipping with fingers or a spatula. Flip once more and let the tortilla finish cooking. Sometimes a few taps with the fingers or slaps with a cloth will help it rise.

TO SERVE
Place the tortillas in a *chiquihuite* (willow basket), cover with a cloth napkin, and serve immediately.

MAKES APPROXIMATELY 30 (2- TO 3-INCH) TORTILLAS

VARIATIONS
To make red tortillas, mix the dough with *chiles anchos* that have been lightly toasted, cleaned, and grated with a bit of water.

CLOCKWISE FROM TOP LEFT

A banana leaf is carefully peeled from the tortilla dough. Tortillas were originally prepared by flattening corn dough by hand on a banana leaf, as shown here.

Today, the dough is flattened between sheets of plastic wrap in a tortilla press. The dough for flour or wheat tortillas is rolled out with a rolling pin on a wooden surface.

LA TORTILLA

TORTILLAS DE HARINA

Flour Tortillas

4¹/₂ cups unbleached flour
  1 teaspoon salt, or to taste
  3 heaping tablespoons vegetable shortening

¹/₂ cup water, approximately (varies depending on quality of flour), at room temperature

Put flour in a glass mixing bowl. Add salt and vegetable shortening. Knead by hand until the mixture has a gritty texture. Add water a little at a time and knead dough until it forms an elastic and shiny ball. If it is too greasy, add a little more flour and water. Set dough aside, covered with a damp cloth, for 30 minutes.

    Pinch off a small ball of dough, and place between 2 sheets of waxed paper. With a rolling pin, roll the ball into a circle about 3 inches in diameter. The tortilla should be very thin. Pull edges with your fingertips, stretching the tortilla a little.

    On a hot thick griddle, cook tortilla on each side for about 2 minutes or until light brown. The tortilla should puff slightly.

    Repeat, using all the dough.

    To serve: Place tortillas in a basket. Serve with cheese or ground meat.

MAKES **20** TORTILLAS

Corn tortillas are common throughout Mexico, but tortillas made from wheat flour, like these Sonoran water tortillas, shown with, clockwise from top right, chiles güeros, chiles piquíns, *and* chiles anchos, *are typical of the North.*

SALSAS ◆ SAUCES

SALSA DE TOMATILLO CON CHILES CASCABELES Y CHILES GUAJILLOS

Tomatillo Sauce with Cascabel and Guajillo Chiles

FOR THE SAUCE
- 1 quart water
- 32 tomatillos, husked
- 6 cloves garlic, peeled
- 1/4 white onion, plus 2 tablespoons minced white onion
- 4 chiles cascabeles or de árbol, lightly fried
- 3 chiles guajillos, seeded, deveined, and lightly fried
- Salt to taste

FOR THE GARNISH
- 2 tablespoons chopped cilantro

Bring water to a boil in a large saucepan. Add tomatillos, 4 garlic cloves, and 1/4 onion. Add chiles cascabeles and guajillos and boil for 20 minutes. Set aside to cool. Drain, discard garlic and onion, and reserve cooking water. Set aside tomatillos and chiles.

Meanwhile, grind remaining 2 garlic cloves in a *molcajete* (classic stone mortar), or put through a press. Add minced onion, and salt to taste. Mix.

Gradually add tomatillos and chiles, and grind well in the molcajete or in a food processor. Add a bit of the cooking water to form a fairly thick sauce, and season to taste.

To serve: Pour green sauce into a molcajete or bowl, and sprinkle with cilantro.

MAKES 1 QUART

Tomatillo Sauce with Cascabel and Guajillo Chiles.

SALSA PICO DE GALLO (SALSA MEXICANA)

Pico de Gallo Sauce (Mexican Sauce)

Pico de Gallo sauce is one of the most popular in Mexico. It is typically served from a clay bowl or stone mortar to accompany fresh tortillas and grilled meats, fowl, fish, or melted cheese.

FOR THE SAUCE
1 1/2 white onions, finely chopped
4 tomatoes (generous 2 pounds), peeled, seeded, and finely chopped
2 to 4 chiles serranos, finely chopped

1/2 cup finely chopped cilantro
Salt to taste
Juice of 1 lime
2 tablespoons olive oil

Combine onion, tomatoes, chiles, and cilantro in a bowl. Season with salt, lime juice, and oil. Stir, and marinate for 1 hour before serving.

Serve with *totopos* (crisply fried tortilla wedges), cheese tacos, quesadillas, or empanadas.

VARIATION: Oregano or chopped avocado may be added to the sauce. Cilantro may be omitted, adding instead freshly ground pepper and chopping the ingredients more coarsely. This version is very popular in Baja California, where it is served with seafood and fried fish.

MAKES 4 TO 5 CUPS

SALSA VERDE

Green Sauce

Green sauce is a classic Mexican hot sauce. It can accompany anything from a tortilla to a cut of broiled meat. In the state of Oaxaca, green sauce is served with pork rind or barbecued meat.

FOR THE SAUCE
1 quart water
12 tomatillos, husked
7 medium cloves garlic, peeled
4 to 8 chiles serranos (vary according to preference for piquancy)

3 tablespoons coarsely chopped white onion
Salt to taste
3/4 cup cilantro leaves, with a bit of stem

FOR THE GARNISH
1/4 cup chopped white onion
1/4 cup chopped cilantro

Bring water to a boil in a saucepan. Add tomatillos, 4 garlic cloves, 4 or more chiles, and onion. Cook over medium heat for 20 minutes, and remove from heat. Drain, and reserve cooking water. Cool.

Meanwhile, purée remaining 3 garlic cloves in a mortar (*molcajete*) or food processor, adding salt to taste. Add cilantro, and blend. Add tomatillo mixture. Add a little cooking water, and blend. The sauce should have a slightly thick consistency. Adjust seasoning.

To serve: Pour green sauce into a molcajete, and garnish with onion and cilantro.

MAKES ABOUT 2 CUPS

SALSA BORRACHA

Drunken Sauce

6 chiles pasillas, washed, seeded, and deveined, lightly fried (substitute dried red California chiles)

6 chiles mulatos, washed, seeded, and deveined, lightly fried (substitute dried red California chiles)

1 1/2 teaspoons salt, or to taste

2 medium white onions, peeled, chopped, and sautéed for 5 minutes in 1/3 cup oil

2 medium white onions, peeled and chopped (raw)

3/4 cup beer, pulque, sparkling wine, or 1 tablespoon tequila, or to taste

2 tablespoons olive oil

1/2 cup finely chopped white onion

Grind all ingredients except olive oil and 1/2 cup chopped onion in a food processor or blender, and season to taste with salt (be careful not to overprocess). Add more liquor if desired. At the last moment before serving, stir in the oil and remaining onion.

MAKES 3 TO 4 CUPS

SALSA DE JITOMATE CRUDA

Fresh Tomato Sauce

2 medium tomatoes, diced

1 medium white onion, diced

8 green onions, finely chopped

12 sprigs cilantro, finely chopped

3 to 6 fresh chiles serranos or 2 chiles jalapeños, minced

Salt to taste

1/3 cup grapefruit or lime juice

1 medium avocado, peeled, pitted, and diced

1 teaspoon fresh oregano, crumbled

Combine all ingredients. If prepared ahead of time, combine all the ingredients except the avocado, which should be added just before serving.

MAKES 3 TO 4 CUPS

In Oaxaca, traditional cooking makes use of the rich variety of local chiles.

SALSA DE ALBAÑILES

Bricklayer's Sauce

1 medium onion, peeled and quartered
2 small garlic cloves, peeled
1 1/2 teaspoons salt or to taste
8 sprigs fresh cilantro, chopped
4 to 6 fresh chiles serranos or 2 to 3 chiles jalapeños, stemmed and roasted whole
1 1/2 cups tomatillos, husked and roasted or boiled in water

1 pinch sugar
1/3 to 1/2 cup water
1 teaspoon salt or to taste

FOR THE GARNISH
1 cup fresh minced cilantro
3/4 cup minced white onion

Combine onion, garlic, and salt in a mortar or food processor. If using a mortar, grind well. If using a processor, pulse once very quickly. It is very important not to overprocess or the texture of the salsa will suffer. Add cilantro and pulse again, very quickly.

Add chiles, tomatillos, sugar, and water, and pulse again. To prepare without a mortar or processor, mince all ingredients extremely fine and combine. Season to taste.

Garnish with chopped cilantro and onion.

MAKES 4 CUPS

SALSA DE TOMATE AL CHIPOTLE

Tomatillo-Chipotle Sauce

1 teaspoon salt or to taste
2 garlic cloves, peeled
4 chiles chipotles or moritas, roasted, seeded, and deveined, if desired, soaked in hot water 10 minutes, or 2 canned pickled chiles chipotles
1 1/2 cups tomatillos, husked and boiled in water

1/2 medium white onion, cooked with tomatillos
10 cilantro sprigs
1/3 medium white onion, chopped
1/3 to 1/2 cup water

FOR THE GARNISH
3/4 cup fresh chopped cilantro

If you are using the classic stone mortar (molcajete), grind salt and garlic first so that their flavors will permeate all the other ingredients. If you are using a food processor, you can still add the ingredients in this order,

but it is extremely important to pulse as quickly as possible when blending so that ingredients will retain a coarse, chunky texture.

Garnish with cilantro.

MAKES 4 CUPS

ANTOJITOS ◆ APPETIZERS

GUACAMOLE DE LA MIXTECA

Guacamole, Mixtec Style

Avocado is a fruit rich in vitamins and believed to have extraordinary medicinal powers. The Oaxaca–Mixteca region is famous for its abundant yields of this fruit.

FOR THE GUACAMOLE
    4 large California avocados, purchased ahead of
        time to allow for ripening, if necessary
        Salt to taste
    1 cup minced white onion
    4 chiles serranos, minced

$1/2$ cup finely chopped cilantro

FOR THE GARNISH
    $1/2$ tomato, diced
    $1/4$ cup minced white onion
    4 to 6 sprigs cilantro, with leaves and a bit of stem

Peel and pit avocados. Mash pulp in a bowl or *molca-jete* (mortar), and add salt to taste. Add onion, chiles, and cilantro. Continue mashing until guacamole is thick and lumpy.

Garnish with tomato, onion, and cilantro. Serve with corn tortillas or *totopos* (crisply fried tortilla wedges).
    Serve immediately.

MAKES ABOUT 3 CUPS

A fourteenth-century Mexican lintel is an appropriate backdrop for Guacamole, Mixtec Style.

TACOS A LA CREMA

Tacos with Cream

When tacos are fried crisp, then covered with cream and cheese, they are often called flautas,
which means "flutes."

FOR THE TACOS
- 24 corn tortillas
- 3 or 4 large potatoes, peeled, cooked in salted water, drained, and mashed
- 2 1/4 pounds Oaxaca, mozzarella, or Monterey Jack cheese sliced in thin strips
- 1 quart vegetable oil

FOR THE GREEN SAUCE
- 1 1/2 quarts water
- 14 tomatillos, husked
- 1 white onion, halved
- 5 cloves garlic, peeled
- 4 chiles serranos
- 1 cup cilantro
- 1 large California avocado, peeled and pitted

Salt to taste

FOR THE RED SAUCE
- 1 1/2 quarts water
- 3 tomatoes (1 3/4 pounds)
- 1 white onion, sliced
- 6 cloves garlic, peeled
- 2 chiles chipotles, 4 chiles serranos, or 2 chiles jalapeños
- Salt to taste

FOR THE GARNISH
- 1/2 cup plus 2 tablespoons crème fraîche
- 1 cup sour cream
- 1/2 cup half-and-half
- 1 1/2 cups feta or fresh cheese, crumbled

Prepare the tacos: Heat tortillas on a comal or griddle. Put some mashed potato and cheese strips off-center on tortillas. Roll, and secure with a toothpick. (The tacos can be prepared ahead of time to this point and stored in a plastic bag in the refrigerator).

Prepare the green sauce: Bring water to a boil in a saucepan. Add tomatillos, 1/2 onion, 3 garlic cloves, and chiles. Boil for 30 minutes. Remove from heat, and cool. Drain, and reserve cooking water. Blend cooked ingredients with remaining 1/2 onion, remaining 2 garlic cloves, cilantro, and avocado in a blender or food processor. Add salt. If sauce becomes too thick, add a little cooking water.

Prepare the red sauce: Bring water to a boil in a saucepan. Add tomatoes, half of the onion slices, 4 garlic cloves, and chiles. Boil for 25 minutes. Drain, and reserve cooking water. Blend cooked ingredients with reserved onion slices and remaining 2 garlic cloves in a blender or food processor. Add salt. Add a little cooking water to make a slightly thick sauce.

Heat oil in a frying pan to just under smoking point. Fry tacos, turning, until crisp. Remove, and drain on paper towels.

To serve: Place 3 tacos on each of 8 plates. Pour green sauce on one side and red sauce on the other. Combine crème fraîche, sour cream, and half-and-half, and pour over tacos. Sprinkle with cheese. Serve with tequila.

MAKES 24 TACOS

Cream- and cheese-covered tacos, which have been stuffed, rolled, and fried, are served on a Tlaxcalteca ceramic dish. The rim of the glass of tequila has been dipped in coarse salt.

EMPANADAS AL ACHIOTE RELLENAS DE CAMARÓN

Shrimp-Stuffed Empanadas with Annatto Seeds

FOR THE DOUGH

- 1 pound, 6 ounces fresh masa or equivalent made with masa harina
- 3 cups plus 6 tablespoons vegetable oil
- 1 tablespoon annatto seeds
- 1 tablespoon prepared annatto seeds (see below)
- 1/2 cup flour
- Salt to taste

FOR THE STUFFING

- 1/2 cup olive oil
- 1 white onion, grated
- 4 cloves garlic, puréed or put through a press
- 2 tomatoes, roasted and puréed
- 2 cups chopped, cooked shrimp
- 2 chiles jalapeños, finely chopped
- 1 teaspoon prepared annatto seeds (see below)
- 1 teaspoon ground allspice
- 1 teaspoon dried oregano, crushed
- Salt to taste

Prepare the dough: Put masa in a large bowl. Set aside.

Heat 6 tablespoons vegetable oil in a skillet, and add annatto seeds. Cook until seeds are soft and almost dissolved. Remove seeds from oil, and add prepared annatto seeds, mixing until a smooth paste is formed.

Add seeds to the masa with flour, a little water, and salt. Knead masa until smooth. Set aside.

Prepare the stuffing: Heat olive oil in a saucepan. Add onion and garlic. Sauté until translucent.

Add tomato purée, shrimp, and chiles. Season with prepared annatto seeds, allspice, oregano, and salt.

Cook until the moisture has evaporated from the mixture. Cool slightly.

Using tortilla press, make tortillas 2 1/2 to 3 inches in diameter from the masa. Spoon stuffing onto tortillas, and fold tortillas in half, sealing edges, to form the empanadas. Cover with plastic wrap. The empanadas can be refrigerated until serving time.

To serve: Fry the empanadas in 3 cups hot oil until golden. Drain on paper towels, and serve immediately. Serve with guacamole (see page 26) or cold tomato sauce.

MAKES ABOUT 20 EMPANADAS

RECADO DE ACHIOTE

Annatto-Seed Seasoning

- 3 tablespoons annatto seeds
- 5 cloves garlic, peeled
- 1 tablespoon black peppercorns
- 1 tablespoon dried oregano, crushed
- 1 white onion, coarsely chopped

Simmer annatto seeds in a little water for 10 minutes. Let stand overnight to soften seeds. Drain. Combine seeds with garlic, peppercorns, oregano, and onion, and grind to a fine consistency in an electric spice grinder or a mortar. Store in a glass jar in the refrigerator.

To use, dissolve seasoning in a little Seville (bitter) orange juice or vinegar or in a mixture of equal amounts of orange and grapefruit juices.

MAKES ABOUT 1/2 cup

CHILE CON ASADERO

Chile with Melted Cheese

*The chiles used in Chihuahua are known as chilacas, or as California or Anaheim chiles,
and are different from chilacas used elsewhere in Mexico. They are roasted,
placed in a plastic bag for a few minutes to ease the peeling procedure, deveined, and sliced into thin strips.
In the northern part of Mexico, asadero is one of the most popular dishes.*

3 1/3 cups vegetable oil
24 California (Anaheim) chiles
1/2 cup butter
3 red onions, finely chopped
8 cups asadero, soft Cheddar, Monterey Jack, or
   Mennonite cheese, cubed

2 cups milk
1 1/2 cups heavy cream
1 1/2 cups crème fraîche
   Salt and pepper to taste
2 large tomatoes, peeled, finely chopped, and well
   drained

Heat 3 cups oil in a frying pan, and fry chiles briefly, until their skins begin to swell. Remove immediately. Place chiles in a plastic bag, and then peel and cut into thin strips.

Heat butter and remaining 1/3 cup oil in a frying pan, and sauté onions. Add chile strips, and sauté. Add cheese, and cook over low heat until cheese begins to melt. Add milk, heavy cream, and crème fraîche, and season with salt and pepper. Cook for 20 minutes or until a thick sauce is formed with the partially melted cheese. Add tomatoes immediately before serving.

To serve: Spoon into individual clay bowls or onto salad plates. Serve with freshly made corn tortillas.

SERVES 8

The ingredients for Chile with Melted Cheese.

AJOS Y CHILES CHIPOTLES A LA OAXAQUEÑA

Garlic and Chipotle Chiles, Oaxaca Style

The smoked flavor of Oaxacan chiles chipotles makes this accompaniment special.

2¼ pounds chiles pasillas or chipotles, washed,
    pierced a few times with a needle, and soaked
    in water for 2 hours
  6 white onions, quartered
  60 cloves garlic, peeled

8 sprigs fresh thyme or 1 teaspoon dried thyme
1 teaspoon whole cloves
2 tablespoons black peppercorns
  Salt to taste
3 quarts mild fruit vinegar

Layer chiles, onion, garlic, thyme, cloves, peppercorns, and salt in a 1½-gallon glass jar. Repeat layers until all ingredients are used. Pour vinegar over layers, and macerate for 4 to 5 days, covered tightly, to pickle thoroughly.

Serve 2 or 3 chiles on a small plate with onion, garlic, and vinegar as an appetizer, or stuff pickled chiles with gefilte fish or fish croquettes. They also can be used in table sauces.

MAKES ABOUT 1 GALLON

Oaxaca is known for its spicy dishes, many of which require a prodigious amount of garlic.

TAMALES OAXAQUEÑOS

Pork and Chicken Tamales

My grandmother Margarita considered Oaxacan-style tamales the most important offering for the altar on the Day of the Dead. These tamales are different from others, since they are steamed in banana leaves rather than corn husks. They are commonly served with Mexican-style coffee or hot atole. If you cannot get banana leaves, you can use corn husks.

FOR THE FILLING
  1 medium chicken, cut in pieces (approximately 2 1/2 pounds)
  1/2 pound pork loin, cut in pieces
  1 medium white onion, peeled and quartered
  6 garlic cloves, peeled
  Salt to taste

FOR THE DOUGH
  2 generous pounds fresh white masa (or masa

prepared with masa harina)
  Salt to taste
  1 1/4 cups water with 1 teaspoon baking soda
  1 pound lard, soft, beaten until fluffy
  6 1/2 cups mole (see page 80)

TO COMPLETE THE TAMALES
  1 1-pound package of banana leaves, cut into twenty-four 8 × 12-inch rectangles

Prepare the filling: Place the chicken, pork, onion, garlic, and salt in a stockpot and add enough water to cover. Simmer gently over medium heat for 45 minutes, then check to see if chicken is done. When chicken is tender, remove from pot, and set aside. Continue cooking pork another 45 minutes or until it is done. Allow pork to cool in the broth, then remove it from the pot. Shred both chicken and pork, and set aside.

Prepare the dough: Place the masa in a large glass mixing bowl. Add salt and the water with baking soda dissolved in it. Beat until the ingredients are well incorporated and the mixture has the consistency of soft dough. Then add the lard and continue beating. Test masa by dropping a bit into a glass of water. If it floats, it is light enough. If not, continue beating. Season with 3 tablespoons of mole.

Assemble the tamales: Drop 1 or 2 tablespoons of dough onto a banana leaf, spreading it with the back of a spoon to form a very thin layer. Place a tablespoon of meat over the dough, then a tablespoon of mole.

Fold the bottom part of the leaf upward, and the top part of the leaf downward toward the center. Press the leaf to keep in place. Then fold both the sides inward to form a square. Double-wrap the tamal with a second banana leaf, to be sure that the filling does not escape or become soggy in the steaming process. Tie the tamal with strips cut from banana leaves.

Prepare a steamer: Pour water into a steamer, adding a coin. The coin will rattle if the water evaporates. Line the bottom of the steamer with banana leaves. Arrange the tamales in the steamer and then cover with extra banana leaves. Steam for 1 1/2 hours. Tamales are done when the cooked dough can be peeled easily from the leaf. If necessary, add more water to the steamer during cooking time. Allow tamales to cool slightly.

To serve: Place the tamales on a large round serving platter, piled high. They can be served for a light dinner, a snack, or for breakfast with black coffee or hot chocolate.

SERVES 8

TAMALITOS REGIOMONTANOS

Small Tamales, Monterrey Style

These small tamales are traditionally served at family reunions.

FOR THE HUSKS
120 dried corn husks, approximately

FOR THE STUFFING
2¹/₂ quarts water
6 cloves garlic, peeled
1 large white onion, coarsely chopped
3 cloves
1 stick cinnamon, about 6 inches long
1³/₄ pounds pork leg or loin, cut in chunks
Salt to taste

FOR THE SAUCE
³/₄ cup lard
2 thick slices white onion
8 chiles anchos, seeded, deveined, and soaked in water for 20 minutes

4 very dry chiles guajillos, lightly roasted, seeded, deveined, and soaked in water for 20 minutes
8 cloves garlic, peeled
1 medium white onion, coarsely chopped
1 teaspoon freshly ground pepper
¹/₂ teaspoon freshly ground allspice
4 bay leaves
1 tablespoon cumin seeds
Salt to taste
2 cups beef broth

FOR THE DOUGH
1¹/₂ pounds lard
2 tablespoons salt, or to taste
3¹/₂ pounds masa or equivalent made with masa harina

Prepare the husks: Fill a stockpot with water, and soak husks overnight. Rinse husks well, and cut off the tip of each. Cut husks in half lengthwise. Dry well with paper towels. Set aside.

Prepare the stuffing: Bring water to a boil in a stockpot. Add garlic, onion, cloves, cinnamon, pork, and salt. Cook over low heat for 2¹/₂ hours or until meat is tender. Cool pork in broth for 2 hours. Shred or finely chop pork, and set aside.

Prepare the sauce: Heat lard in a heavy saucepan. Add onion slices, and sauté. Meanwhile, drain chiles, reserving soaking water. In a blender, purée chiles anchos and guajillos, garlic, onion, pepper, allspice, bay leaves, cumin, and ¹/₂ cup soaking water. Add chile mixture to lard, and simmer for 45 minutes. Add salt, and continue cooking until the sauce thickens. Add shredded pork and beef broth. Continue cooking for 25 minutes.

Prepare the dough: Beat lard with an electric mixer or by hand until light and spongy. Add salt and masa. Beat or knead with a little water or stock until dough is light. The dough is light enough when a small amount floats when dropped in water.

Put 1¹/₂ teaspoons of dough in the center of a corn husk. With the back of a spoon, spread evenly almost to the edges. Line 1 teaspoon of stuffing down the center. Fold sides of husks toward the center, overlapping. Fold top and bottom toward the center. Tie with thin strips cut from corn husks.

Bring 3 cups water to a boil in a steamer base. Drop a coin into the water. When you can no longer

OPPOSITE
Tamales wrapped in banana leaves, Oaxaca style, and in corn husks, lying on a bed of banana leaves.

hear the coin rattling, the water has evaporated. Add more water. Put rack in steamer, and cover with a layer of corn husks.

Place tamales on husks in steamer, standing upright. Cover with a layer of corn husks and a dish towel. Put lid on steamer, and steam for 1½ hours or until the husk can be easily peeled from the dough. If necessary, add more water to steamer, being careful it does not boil onto tamales.

To serve: Arrange tamales, steaming hot, on a platter. Serve with black coffee, whipped hot chocolate, or atole.

MAKES ABOUT 60 TO 80 TAMALES

TOSTADITAS TURULAS

Mini Shrimp Tostadas

FOR THE DOUGH
1¼ pounds fresh masa or equivalent made with masa harina
⅓ cup warm water
½ cup vegetable oil or lard
½ teaspoon salt

FOR THE SHRIMP
32 small dried shrimp, shelled, or 32 fresh baby shrimp, cooked

FOR THE SAUCE
1 small white onion, finely chopped
2 tomatoes, peeled and finely chopped
2 or 3 chiles serranos, finely chopped
2 tablespoons finely chopped cilantro
¼ cup freshly chopped oregano, or 3/4 teaspoon dried oregano
Salt to taste
Juice of 1 lime

Prepare the dough: Put masa in a bowl, and add water, oil, and salt. Knead for a maximum of 3 minutes.

Heat a comal or griddle for 20 minutes, and prepare a tortilla press. Form 24 balls, 1½ inches in diameter, from the masa, and make tortillas. Cook on the comal until crisp. Keep warm.

Prepare the shrimp: If dried shrimp are salty, soak in cold water for 10 minutes. Drain well. Set aside.

Prepare the sauce: Combine onion, tomato, chiles, and cilantro in a bowl. Season with oregano and salt, and mix. Add lime juice.

To assemble the tostaditas: Place shrimp on top of tortillas, and cover with tomato sauce. Serve 3 tostaditas on each of 8 plates.

MAKES 24 TOSTADITAS

OPPOSITE
For a light lunch or an appetizer, dried shrimp are placed on tortillas and covered with tomato sauce.

Chilapitas

The chilapita *is named after an important city in Guerrero. The Nahuatl Indian word means "river near the chile field." This dish can be served with bean, chicken, sausage, or other stuffings.*

FOR THE DOUGH

2¹/₂ pounds masa made with masa harina

2 tablespoons flour

¹/₂ teaspoon baking powder

1 teaspoon salt

1¹/₂ cups lard

1¹/₂ cups vegetable oil

FOR THE STUFFING

2 chicken breasts, poached and finely shredded

1¹/₂ cups crème fraîche

1 cup finely chopped avocado

24 canned chile chipotle strips

48 slices white onion, thinly sliced on the diagonal

Prepare the masa and add the flour, baking powder, and salt. Knead until the dough is smooth. Divide masa into 24 balls, measuring about 2 inches in diameter. With your fingers, shape into little baskets or bowls, using a greased bowl as a mold. Fry dough in lard and oil until dark yellow. Remove, and drain on paper towels.

Serve hot, filling with chicken and garnishing with cream, avocado, chile strips, and onion.

MAKES 24 CHILAPITAS

Chilapitas are served with green pozole in Guerrero pottery.

PICADITAS DEL PUERTO

Port Picaditas

We used to visit the port of Veracruz for Independence Day holiday whenever we had the time.
I remember the streets lined with open-air food stalls offering a wide variety of local snacks.
This is a common snack served in the harbor.

FOR THE PICADITAS
1 3/4 pounds fresh corn masa or masa made with
  masa harina
1/3 to 1/2 cup hot water
  Salt to taste

FOR THE SAUCE
15 tomatillos, husked
1/2 medium white onion, peeled, and quartered
4 garlic cloves, peeled

4 to 6 chiles de árbol or other small hot dried
  chiles, fried
  Salt to taste
1/2 medium white onion, peeled, and finely chopped

FOR THE FILLING
3/4 cup vegetable oil or lard
1 large white onion, peeled, and finely chopped
3 cups refried beans
2 cups fresh, feta, or farmer's cheese, crumbled

Prepare the picaditas: Heat a comal or griddle. Meanwhile, knead the corn masa, adding the hot water and salt, until it forms a smooth dough. Line a tortilla press with two squares of plastic. Pinch off about 1 tablespoon of the masa dough and shape into a ball. Place the ball on the tortilla press and press slightly with the lever to make a small round tortilla, about 1/4 inch thick, and 2 1/2 to 3 inches in diameter. Carefully peel off the plastic and place dough directly on the preheated comal. Cook until slightly brown, then turn over to cook evenly. Pinch the edge all the way around to form a rim, then pinch the center of the tortilla flat, being careful not to perforate it. Repeat this procedure with remaining masa. Keep picaditas warm by wrapping in a cloth or cloth napkin.

Prepare the sauce: Place tomatillos, onion, and 2 cloves garlic in a medium saucepan. Add enough water to cover and cook over medium heat for about 20 to 25 minutes. Remove from heat and drain; set aside to cool. Place the chiles in a molcajete, blender, or food processor and purée. Add the cooked tomatillos, chopped onion, and remaining 2 cloves garlic, and purée once again. If necessary, add more water, and adjust seasoning.

To assemble the picaditas: Place picaditas on a hot comal or skillet to reheat. Sprinkle with oil, chopped onion, beans, sauce, and cheese. Heat for about 4 minutes.

Serve hot.

SERVES 8

NOTE:
Picaditas are also called *sopes* or *sopecitos* in central Mexico,
pelliscadas in Veracruz, and *memelas* in Oaxaca.

SALPICÓN DE JAIBA

Shredded Crab

Shredded crab is usually served before lunch as an appetizer, and in Mexico, appetizers are an institution. No gathering—public or private, with family or with friends, for business or for pleasure—is considered complete without an hors d'oeuvre. This recipe is from Pardino's restaurant in the port of Veracruz.

3/4 cup olive oil
6 tablespoons butter
6 cloves garlic, chopped
2 white onions, chopped
4 canned chiles jalapeños, chopped
1/2 cup chile juice, reserved from can

1/3 cup canned pickled carrots, chopped
4 medium tomatoes, chopped
1/2 cup chopped parsley
1/2 cup chopped cilantro
Salt and pepper to taste
2 1/2 generous pounds crab meat, cleaned

Heat oil and butter in a frying pan. Add garlic and onion, and sauté.

Add chiles, chile juice, carrots, tomatoes, parsley, and cilantro. Season with salt and pepper, and cook over low heat until mixture thickens, about 25 minutes.

Add crab meat, and sauté until mixture thickens.

Adjust seasonings.

To serve: Place crab on a platter. Serve with freshly made tortillas to roll into tacos.

The shredded crab may also be served in crab shells, sprinkled with bread crumbs, melted butter, and parsley, and baked in a hot oven for 25 minutes.

SERVES 8

A fresh seafood bar in the port of Veracruz.

Crab meat is prepared in a variety of ways—breaded and fried, shredded and sautéed, or simply boiled.

CHILES EN NOGADA

Stuffed Chiles in Walnut Sauce

This famous dish, native to Puebla, commemorates Independence Day, August 21, 1821.
It honors General Agustín de Itúrbide's defeat of the French, and its colors are those of the Mexican flag—
green, white, and red.

FOR THE STUFFING

1/2 cup butter
1 cup olive oil
12 cloves garlic, peeled, plus 10 cloves garlic, minced
2 large white onions, grated
1 pound ground pork
1 pound ground veal
1 pound ground beef
1 pound ground ham
1 cup raisins or currants
2 1/2 cups prunes, pitted and finely chopped
1 1/2 cups candied citron, finely chopped
1 cup dried apricots, finely chopped
6 large pears, finely chopped
6 peaches, finely chopped
4 apples, finely chopped
2 cups pineapple, finely chopped
1 plantain, finely chopped
6 large tomatoes (about 3 1/2 pounds), finely chopped
1 tablespoon ground cinnamon
1/2 teaspoon ground cloves
1/2 teaspoon ground nutmeg
10 bay leaves
6 sprigs thyme
6 sprigs marjoram
1 1/2 tablespoons freshly ground pepper
1 cup dry sherry
1 cup dry white wine
Salt to taste

FOR THE CHILES

32 medium chiles poblanos, roasted, seeded,
deveined, and soaked in salted water and vinegar for 6 hours
2 cups flour

FOR THE BATTER

20 eggs, separated
2 tablespoons salt
6 tablespoons flour
3 quarts vegetable oil

FOR THE SAUCE (WHEN FRESH WALNUTS ARE USED)

4 cups shelled walnuts
1 1/2 cups raw almonds, skinned
14 ounces cream cheese
7 ounces goat cheese
3 ounces fresh cheese, such as feta
1 slice bread trimmed, and soaked in a little milk
2 cups heavy cream, or 1 cup heavy cream mixed with 1 cup half-and-half
1 cup milk
1 tablespoon grated white onion
2 tablespoons sugar
1 teaspoon ground cinnamon
1/2 cup dry sherry
Salt to taste

FOR THE SAUCE (WHEN PACKAGED WALNUTS ARE USED)

4 cups shelled walnuts, soaked in cold water overnight
3 cups shelled raw almonds
14 ounces cream cheese
7 ounces goat cheese
2 cups heavy cream
1 cup half-and-half
2 cups milk

    2 tablespoons grated white onion
³/4 tablespoon ground cinnamon
¹/2 cup dry sherry
    Salt to taste

Prepare the stuffing: Heat butter and oil in a saucepan. Brown 12 garlic cloves, and discard. Brown minced garlic with onion. Add ground meats, and sauté until no longer red. Stir in raisins, prunes, citron, apricots, pears, peaches, apples, pineapple, plantain, and tomatoes. Cook until mixture begins to thicken, about 30 minutes.

Add cinnamon, cloves, nutmeg, bay leaves, thyme, marjoram, pepper, sherry, and white wine. Salt to taste. Simmer, stirring constantly, until the mixture thickens, about 1¹/4 hours. Cool.

Fill prepared chiles with cooled stuffing. Put flour on a piece of waxed paper. Roll chiles in flour, and place on a tray. Cover and refrigerate.

Prepare the batter: Make batter in 3 batches, as needed, or it will not remain fluffy. Beat one-third of egg whites with a little salt until stiff. Lightly beat one-third of egg yolks. Add yolks and 2 tablespoons flour to whites, folding in carefully.

FOR THE GARNISH
    Seeds from 6 pomegranates
    1 bunch parsley, chopped

Meanwhile, heat oil in a deep frying pan. Dip flour-coated chiles in batter, one at a time, and fry over medium heat. Do not crowd pan. Remove, and drain on paper towels.

Prepare the sauce: Boil walnuts in water to cover for 5 minutes. Remove from water. Peel skins. (Or soak walnuts in cold water overnight. Peel.) Boil almonds in water to cover for 25 minutes, and soak in cold water. Peel skins. Grind walnuts and almonds in a blender or food processor, adding cream cheese, goat cheese, feta cheese, bread, cream, milk, onion, sugar, cinnamon, sherry, and salt. The mixture will be very thick. Refrigerate.

If you are using packaged nuts, wash walnuts and almonds, and follow the procedure for fresh nuts.

To serve: Place cold fried chiles on a platter. Ladle walnut sauce on top. Sprinkle with pomegranate seeds, and garnish with parsley.

SERVES 16

NOTE
There may be leftover stuffing, depending on the size of the chiles. It can be used to stuff empanadas, quesadillas, tacos, or poultry. It can be frozen.

OVERLEAF
Stuffed Chiles in Walnut Sauce, which is garnished with pomegranate seeds, is one of the best known dishes from Puebla.

ENSALADAS ◆ SALADS

ENSALADA DE ALCACHOFA
CON FLOR DE CALABAZA, CILANTRO Y ALBAHACA

Artichoke Salad with Squash Blossoms and Cilantro-Basil Dressing

The combination of cilantro and basil complements the flavor of fresh artichokes in this modern recipe.
Squash blossoms are eaten uncooked—an unusual touch.

FOR THE ARTICHOKES
   6 quarts water
      Salt to taste
   8 large artichokes

FOR THE VINAIGRETTE
   3/4 cup mild cider vinegar
      Salt to taste
   1 teaspoon freshly ground pepper
   1 tablespoon sugar

   1 cup chopped fresh basil, or 1/3 cup dried basil
   1 cup chopped cilantro
   3 cloves garlic, chopped
   1 cup olive oil
   1 cup corn oil

FOR THE GARNISH
   48 squash blossoms, washed, cleaned, and thick
      outer leaves removed

Prepare the artichokes: Bring water to a boil in a large saucepan. Add salt. When water is at a rolling boil, add artichokes. Boil for 40 minutes or until the leaves can be easily removed. Remove from water, and cool.

Prepare the vinaigrette: Blend vinegar, salt, pepper, sugar, basil, cilantro, garlic, and olive and corn oils in a blender or food processor for 4 minutes. Test for seasoning. Refrigerate for 1 hour.

To serve: Place 6 large artichoke leaves on each of 8 plates. Center artichoke bottom on the plate. Arrange 6 squash blossoms on each plate (see photo). Pour vinaigrette over artichokes, or serve dressing in a bowl.

SERVES 8

RIGHT
The markets in Mexico City offer a variety of fresh produce for salads. Squash blossoms and artichokes are combined with a cilantro and basil dressing.

OPPOSITE
Squash blossoms can be used in salads, in a stuffing for crêpes, or as a basic ingredient in a savory soup.

ENSALADA DE NARANJA, JÍCAMA Y CILANTRO

Orange, Jícama, and Cilantro Salad

FOR THE SALAD
   16 seedless oranges
   2 red onions, finely chopped
   1 large jícama, finely chopped, or 2 cups finely
      chopped water chestnuts
   1 1/2 cups cilantro, chopped
      Salt to taste

Chile piquín or any very hot red dried chile,
   finely ground, to taste

FOR THE GARNISH
   1 cup cilantro leaves
   1 red onion, thinly sliced

Peel the oranges, and thinly slice crosswise into rounds. Place half the slices on a platter. Layer half the onion, half the jícama, and half the cilantro on the orange.

Repeat layers of orange, onion, jícama, and cilantro. Season with salt and chile. Garnish with cilantro leaves and onion. Refrigerate for 2 hours.

SERVES 8

ENSALADA DE VERDOLAGA Y CHILES DE AGUA CON QUESO DE CABRA

Purslane and Chiles de Agua Salad with Goat Cheese

Native to Mexico, purslane has both wild and domestic varieties. The domestic is distinguished by the size of its leaf and its color. Purslane is eaten in salads and in green and red moles (casseroles and stews), or with pork.

FOR THE VINAIGRETTE
   4 cloves garlic, crushed
   1 teaspoon black peppercorns
      Juice of 6 large limes
   3/4 tablespoon salt (or to taste)
   3/4 cup corn oil
   1/2 cup olive oil
   1/3 cup sunflower oil
   1/3 to 1/2 cup chopped chives

FOR THE SALAD
1 3/4 pounds purslane or watercress

16 chiles de agua or wax peppers, roasted, left to
   sweat slightly, deveined (soaked for a few hours
   in icewater if they are very spicy), and cut into
   thin strips
   1/3 cup oil
      Salt and pepper to taste

FOR THE GARNISH
   2 goat cheeses (1 white and 1 ash-coated), cut
      into 8 pieces and refrigerated for 6 hours or
      over night
   1 bunch of chives, cut at the tips and ends

To prepare the vinaigrette: In a large stone or pottery mortar, crush the garlic cloves. Add the peppercorns and crush them into small pieces. Add the lime juice and salt, and mix well. Add the oils, a little at a time, and mix until smooth. Add the chives.

   To prepare the salad: Clean and wash the

purslane. Pat dry and refrigerate for 3 hours. Refrigerate the chile strips. When ready to serve, heat the oil and sauté the chiles over medium heat until wilted, about 1 to 2 minutes. Sprinkle them with salt and pepper. Drain after cooking.

To serve: Spoon a little vinaigrette onto each plate. Top with a small mound of the purslane and press lightly. Place the chile strips and the cheese slices on the side. Garnish with the chives. Just before serving, baste each salad with a bit more vinaigrette. Serve with sesame bread sticks.

SERVES 8

The combination of the light-colored, roasted chiles with lemon vinaigrette and goat cheese gives a special touch to this exquisite Mexican vegetable. (Note: If purslane is unavailable, watercress is a good substitute.)

ENSALADA DE AROMAS

Scented Salad

*Tlilxóchil, a black flower cultivated by the Totonacas, captivated the great warrior Tlacaelel, who was seduced
by its scent. The dried sheath of this flower was transformed into a fundamental element to add scent to the foods of
our ancestors. Today, vanilla continues to be a unique ingredient due to its magnificent essence.*

FOR THE VINAIGRETTE
   1/4 cup finely chopped purple onion or shallot
   3 cloves garlic, finely chopped
   1 teaspoon freshly ground pepper
   1 1/2 teaspoons salt
   1 teaspoon sugar
   4 vanilla beans, finely chopped or ground
   3 tablespoons pure vanilla extract
   1/2 wine or cider vinegar
   3/4 cup Italian olive oil
   3/4 cup Spanish olive oil

FOR THE SALAD
   10 cups water
   1 1/2 tablespoons salt
   1 bunch huanzontles (cut tender flowers), or tiny
      broccoli
   4 lobster tails
   16 thin slices fresh (panela) or mozzarella cheese
   2 ripe avocados

FOR THE GARNISH
   3 ounces caviar

Prepare the vinaigrette: In a bowl, combine onion and chopped garlic. Add the pepper, salt, sugar, vanilla beans, and extract. Add the vinegar and mix well until the salt is dissolved. Add oil gradually, and whisk until smooth. Transfer to an airtight container and refrigerate for 2 days.

Prepare the salad: In a saucepan, bring 5 cups water to a boil with 3/4 tablespoon salt. Meanwhile, cut huanzontle flowers and cook them in small portions so they are soft and do not turn yellow. Drain and soak them in cold water for a few seconds. Drain again, pat dry, and refrigerate for 15 minutes. In another saucepan, bring 5 cups water to a boil, add remaining salt, and cook the lobsters for 6 to 8 minutes. Drain

lobsters and cool in cold water. With a sharp knife or scissors, cut down the middle and remove shells. Slice crosswise. If you are using crawfish, cook in boiling water for 4 minutes and drain (they can be cooked with or without shell). Halve avocados. Remove pit with a sharp knife. Peel and thinly slice each half, arranging into a fan shape.

To serve: Refrigerate 8 large plates. Place a large bunch of huanzontles in the middle of each plate. Place lobster or crawfish slices on one side and cheese strips on the other side to form a cross. Place avocado slices next to the cheese, pressing carefully to obtain a fan pattern. Garnish with caviar. Sprinkle vinaigrette over salad.

VARIATIONS
Place a slice of roasted chile poblano over the seafood. You can also serve
this salad with scallops or langostines sautéed in butter.

SERVES 8

OPPOSITE
The addition of vanilla enhances the sweetness of the main ingredients of this salad—lobster, cheese, and avocados.

SOPAS ◆ SOUPS

SOPA DE HONGOS SILVESTRES

Wild Mushroom Soup

Mushroom soup prepared with epazote, cilantro, and fresh chiles is a must in Mexico.
On the other hand, dried mushrooms are used for filling quesadillas that are fried or prepared on the comal.

FOR THE CHICKEN STOCK
- 4 chicken wings
- 2 chicken thighs with legs
- 1 large onion, cut into 4 wedges
- 2 heads garlic, separated into cloves
- 3 carrots, peeled
- 4 stalks celery, chopped
- 1/2 leek, chopped
- 2 turnips, peeled and chopped
- 8 whole peppercorns
- 3 quarts water

FOR THE SOUP
- 1/3 cup oil
- 1/3 cup butter
- 2 onions, grated
- 6 cloves garlic, finely chopped
- 6 green chiles, finely chopped
- 2 1/2 pounds wild mushrooms, finely chopped, either clavito, señorita, yema, pata de pájaro (bird's foot), seta, morilla, or a combination
- 5 ripe tomatoes (approximately 2 1/2 pounds), peeled and chopped
- 3/4 cup epazote, finely chopped
- Salt and pepper to taste

Prepare the chicken stock: In a kettle, put the wings and thighs, onion, garlic, carrots, celery, leek, turnips, and peppercorns. Add water and bring to a boil. Lower heat and simmer the broth for 1 1/2 hours. Skim the fat and strain. Reserve chicken for another use.

Prepare the soup: In a large saucepan, heat the oil and butter. Add the onions, garlic, green chiles, wild mushrooms, tomatoes, and epazote, and cook until mixture thickens. Season with salt and pepper. Heat the stock and add it slowly.

Serve the soup piping hot. Or serve it from a bowl to which 1 1/2 cups heavy cream have been added.

VARIATION
Serve the soup with thin chile strips or add 1 1/2 pounds pumpkin or squash flowers.

SERVES 8

OPPOSITE
The nutritive value of mushrooms has been known since pre-Hispanic times.
Among those varieties found in Mexico are clavitos (little nails), señoritas, bermellones (porcini), setas doradas,
and setas azules (cèpes), as well as yemas (buds) and morillas (morels).

POZOLE JALISCIENSE

Pork and Hominy Soup, Jalisco Style

This hearty pork soup is enjoyed throughout Mexico. Jalisco has two versions: white and red.
Since pozole contains meat, corn, and vegetables, it is considered a meal in itself and often is served alone.

FOR THE CORN BASE
4 1/2 quarts water
3 tablespoons ground limestone
2 white onions, halved
2 1/4 pounds dried corn kernels

FOR THE SOUP
10 quarts water
2 heads garlic, halved
2 white onions, halved
2 1/4 pounds pig's head, chopped
2 pork soup bones, preferably shoulder hocks
2 pig's feet, cleaned and halved
1 pound fatback

2 1/4 pounds boneless pork loin, in chunks
1 2 1/4—pound hen or frying chicken, in pieces
Salt to taste

FOR THE GARNISH
1 head lettuce, shredded
1 1/2 bunches radishes, sliced or diced
3 large white onions, finely chopped
2 1/2 to 3 ounces ground chile piquín
2 1/2 to 3 ounces dried oregano, crushed
48 stale corn tortillas, fried in oil until crisp
2 California avocados, peeled, pitted, and sliced
8 limes, halved

Prepare the corn base: Bring water to a boil in a large saucepan. Add limestone, onions, and corn, and cook over low heat until corn is tender. Remove corn, and cool. Wash and remove skin from kernels.

Prepare the soup: Heat water in a large saucepan. Add corn and garlic. Cook until corn swells; remove gar-lic, and discard. Add onion, pork meats, fatback, and hen. Add salt to taste. Cook over medium heat for 1 1/2 hours or until meat is tender. If necessary, add more water.

To serve: Ladle pozole into soup bowls. Serve lettuce, radishes, onion, chile, oregano, tortillas, avocado, and lime in bowls on the side.

SERVES 16

SOPA VERDE

Green Soup

FOR THE SOUP
  5 quarts water
  2 fish heads, preferably red snapper, sea bass, or
    grouper, washed
  1 fish backbone, washed
  1 fish tail, washed
  1 cup dry white wine
  4 medium carrots, peeled
  1/2 leek, in 4 pieces
  1 small turnip
  1 white onion, quartered
  4 cloves garlic, peeled
  10 sprigs parsley
  4 bay leaves
  10 black peppercorns
  2 tablespoons powdered chicken bouillon, or salt
    to taste

FOR THE SAUCE
  6 chiles poblanos, seeded, deveined, and chopped
  2 cups chopped parsley
  1 1/2 cups chopped cilantro
  1/2 cup epazote, or to taste
  1/2 cup puréed white onion
  6 cloves garlic, peeled
  1/3 cup oil
  5 1/3 tablespoons butter
    Salt and pepper to taste
  2 1/2 pounds medium shrimp

FOR THE GARNISH
  8 limes, halved

Prepare the soup: Bring water to a boil in a stockpot. Add fish heads, backbone, and tail. Stir in wine, carrots, leek, turnip, onion, garlic, parsley, bay leaves, peppercorns, and bouillon. Cook over low heat for 1 1/4 hours. Cool.

Strain broth, reserving vegetables. Purée about one-quarter of the vegetables in a blender or food processor. Add to broth, and stir. Heat to a boiling point, and hold.

Prepare the sauce: Purée chiles, parsley, cilantro, epazote, onion, and garlic with 3 cups of the fish broth in a blender or food processor. Heat oil and butter in a saucepan. Add blended ingredients, and cook until thick. Add salt and pepper to taste. Stir in boiling broth, and adjust seasoning. Simmer for 25 minutes. Add the shrimp during the last 5 minutes of cooking.

Serve green soup from a tureen, with lime halves on the side.

SERVES 8

OVERLEAF
Mexican cooks rely on clay cookware.
Green Soup is served from a clay tureen from Michoacán.

SOPA DE CAMARÓN RINCONADA

Shrimp Soup, Rinconada Style

In Rinconada, a small village between the cities of Veracruz and Xalapa, food stands and restaurants serve this delicious shrimp soup as a hearty breakfast.

FOR THE SOUP
- ²/₃ cup olive oil
- 4 medium white onions, sliced on the diagonal
- 6 large tomatoes, finely chopped
- Salt to taste
- 4 chiles jalapeños, sliced
- 2 quarts fish stock

- 3 sprigs epazote or cilantro, or 1 teaspoon dried oregano
- 2¹/₂ pounds small shrimp, preferably fresh-water, unshelled

FOR THE GARNISH
- 8 limes, sliced in wedges

Prepare the soup: Heat oil in a large saucepan or stock-pot. Add onion, and sauté. Add tomatoes, and simmer until mixture begins to thicken. Season with salt. Add chiles and fish stock. When mixture begins to boil, add epazote and shrimp. Continue cooking over medium heat for 15 minutes.

To serve: Divide shrimp among 8 soup bowls, and fill each bowl with soup. Garnish with limes. Serve with cold beer.

SERVES 8

LEFT
Freshly boiled shrimp for peeling.

OPPOSITE
Shrimp Soup, Rinconada Style

CALDO GALLEGO A LA MEXICANA

Meat and Vegetable Stew with Chiles, Saffron, and Chorizo

My mother often prepared this soup for Sunday meals, in memory of my late grandfather Miguel.
He was of Spanish origin and always liked hearty Spanish-style dishes such as this one.
He didn't care that mother had adapted it to the Mexican way of cooking.

1 pound small white navy beans or garbanzos (chick-peas), soaked overnight if desired
4 bay leaves
1 teaspoon dried thyme
1 teaspoon dried marjoram
12 garlic cloves, peeled
1 medium white onion, peeled and quartered
1 teaspoon lightly toasted saffron
2 cups white wine
4 to 5 quarts water
7 ounces thickly sliced bacon, diced
1 1/2 pounds boneless veal, cut in chunks
2 1/4 pounds pork hock, cut in chunks
1 thick smoked pork rib, cut in pieces
10 ounces ham, cut in pieces
4 chicken breasts, boned and cut in pieces
3 large tomatoes
3 chiles de árbol or other small hot dried chile,

washed, seeded, and deveined, lightly toasted
3 chiles guajillos or California chiles, or dried red New Mexican chiles, washed, seeded, and deveined, lightly toasted
2 medium white onions, peeled and quartered
1/3 cup olive oil
3 large chorizo sausages
3/4 pound Viennese or Catalán chorizo sausage
4 smoked pork ribs
1 1/2 pounds fresh Swiss chard, mild kale, or other greens, thoroughly rinsed and chopped
1 medium head cabbage, halved, cored, and quartered
1 pound baby potatoes, cooked
1 cup chopped parsley
2 tablespoons powdered chicken bouillon or salt to taste
2 tablespoons sugar or to taste

Prepare the soup: Combine the navy beans, bay leaves, thyme, marjoram, 6 cloves garlic, onion, saffron, wine, water, bacon, veal, pork hock, pork rib, ham, and chicken breasts in a large stockpot or saucepan and simmer until the meat is tender.

Place the tomatoes, chiles de árbol and guajillos, onions, and remaining 6 cloves garlic in a blender or food processor and blend into a smooth sauce. Heat the oil in a heavy pan and add the sauce. Cook for 45 minutes or until it renders its fat. Then add to the soup.

Fry the sausages and ribs until light brown. Drain off fat, and add meats to soup. Add Swiss chard, cabbage, potatoes, and parsley. Adjust seasoning and add bouillon and sugar to taste. Simmer 25 minutes.

To serve: Serve hot from a tureen.

SERVES 12 TO 16

PASTAS ◆ PASTAS

PASTA CON HONGOS DE TEMPORADA AL MIL TOMATE CON CHILE MORITA

Pasta with Mushroom-Tomatillo Sauce

Dozens of varieties of mushrooms grow in Mexico, ranging from tiny to huge in size, subtle to strong in flavor. This recipe may be prepared with any variety of mushroom available.

FOR THE SAUCE

4 cups water

1 1/2 pounds mil tomates (tiny tomatillos) or 1 1/2 pounds regular tomatillos, husked

1/2 medium white onion, peeled and quartered

8 cloves garlic, peeled

1 pound tomatillos, ripe, almost yellow, husked and roasted

1/2 medium white onion, peeled and roasted

4 cloves garlic, peeled and roasted

5 to 8 chiles moritas or chipotles, roasted whole and soaked in hot water 10 to 15 minutes (you may substitute canned chipotles or other small, hot chiles, fresh or dried)

1 medium white onion, peeled and quartered

2/3 cup vegetable oil

1 1/4 to 1 1/2 pounds mushrooms, washed and sliced

Salt to taste

Prepare the sauce: Bring water to a boil in a medium saucepan. Add mil tomates, onion, 4 cloves raw garlic, and boil for 15 minutes. In a blender or food processor, combine the boiled ingredients, 1 cup of the cooking liquid, the roasted tomatillos, roasted onion, roasted garlic, roasted chiles moritas, and quartered raw onion. Purée, dividing the mixture into batches if necessary.

Meanwhile, heat oil in a medium saucepan. Add remaining 4 cloves of raw garlic and brown. Stir in mushrooms and sauté. Add sauce and season with salt to taste. Simmer until the mixture renders its fat, about one hour.

To serve with pasta (cooked *al dente*): Add 1/2 cup butter as you combine the pasta with the sauce. Garnish with fried chiles moritas.

To serve as a taco filling: Serve with freshly made blue-corn tortillas. To thin the sauce, add water or chicken broth. Kept thick, the sauce is also a good filling for quesadillas or omelets.

SERVES 8

Guajillo Chile Fettuccine

*Parmesan cheese is one of the lowest in cholesterol, but it must be taken into account that
one tablespoon of Parmesan contains 28 calories and 1.8 grams of fat.
For this reason, those watching their weight should use Parmesan in moderation.*

FOR THE SAUCE
- 3 tablespoons butter
- 1 1/2 cups extra-virgin olive oil
- Salt to taste
- 1 1/3 cups finely chopped garlic
- 24 chiles guajillos or Chimayos, washed, deveined, and finely chopped
- 1 1/2 teaspoons salt or powdered consommé
- 1/2 teaspoon freshly ground pepper

FOR THE PASTA
- 2 tablespoons corn oil
- 1/2 onion, cut into two quarters
- Salt or powdered consommé to taste
- 2 pounds thin fettuccine

FOR THE GARNISH
- 1/2 pound freshly grated Parmesan

Prepare the sauce: In a saucepan, heat the butter, olive oil, and salt. Add garlic and cook for 3 minutes. Add chiles and continue to cook, stirring constantly, until the garlic is golden brown. Season with salt and pepper to taste.

Prepare the pasta: In a large saucepan of boiling water, add the 2 tablespoons of oil, onion, and salt. Bring to a rolling boil, add pasta, and cook for 8 minutes or to desired tenderness. Drain in a colander; remove and discard the onion.

To serve: Using tongs, mix the fettuccine into the oil prepared with the chiles. Transfer the pasta to a warm serving platter and sprinkle with the Parmesan. Serve immediately.

SERVES 8 TO 10

*Guajillo chiles make a hearty, satisfying sauce
that will delight pasta lovers.*

PLATOS FUERTES

◆

MAIN COURSES

FILETE AL CHIPOTLE

Beef Filet with Chipotle Chile

FOR THE SAUCE
- 3/4 cup vegetable oil
- 3 to 6 dried, or 2 canned, chiles chipotles
- 1 chile ancho
- 1 1/2 white onions, quartered
- 4 medium cloves garlic, peeled
- Salt to taste
- 25 fresh or canned tomatillos, husked
- 1/2 cup chopped cilantro
- 1/3 cup olive oil or corn oil
- 2 thick slices white onion

FOR THE BEEF
- 2 tablespoons butter
- 1/2 cup olive oil
- 8 beef filets (filet mignon), 5 to 6 ounces each
- Salt to taste
- 3/4 tablespoon freshly ground pepper
- 1 1/2 cups beef broth

FOR THE GARNISH
- 8 tortillas, 4 inches in diameter, fried in oil
- 8 slices manchego or Monterey Jack cheese, 3 ounces each
- Chopped cilantro

Prepare the sauce: Heat vegetable oil in a frying pan. Fry chiles chipotles and ancho briefly. Remove, and drain. Add onion and garlic to oil, and brown. Salt to taste. Add tomatillos, which have been boiled in 3 cups water for 15 minutes (or briefly if using canned). Add more oil if necessary. Remove from heat, and pour mixture into a blender. Add cilantro, and blend.

Heat olive oil in a frying pan, and brown onion slices. Remove onion when brown, and discard. Add sauce, and cook over low heat for 40 minutes or until fat rises to the surface. Adjust seasoning. Keep warm.

Prepare the beef: Heat a heavy, dry frying pan for 25 minutes. Add a little butter and oil. Heat. Brown 4 filets, frying for 3 to 4 minutes on a side and turning once. When juice begins to rise to the surface, sprinkle with salt and pepper. Remove from skillet and keep warm. Repeat procedure with remaining 4 filets. Add chicken broth to pan juices and boil until reduced by half. Add sauce, and simmer for 25 minutes. Add meat to sauce, and heat for 5 to 8 minutes.

To serve: Place 1 tortilla on each plate. Place 1 filet on the tortilla, and top with 1 cheese slice. Slip under broiler to melt cheese. Cover with hot sauce, and sprinkle with cilantro. Serve with refried beans.

SERVES 8

OPPOSITE
*Mexican kitchenware and table linen are often excellent examples
of Indian handcraft. The Tarahumaran jug complements a serape on the chair,
in a table setting for Beef Filet with Chipotle Chile.*

TOURNEDOS CON MORILLAS A LA CREMA Y CHILE VERDE

Tournedos with Morels in Chile-Cream Sauce

*Years of research in Mexican cuisine and the combination of indigenous
ingredients have resulted in a repertoire of recipes which I serve at special feasts.
This delicious meat dish is a fine main course at a wedding dinner.*

FOR THE MARINADE
- 4 garlic cloves, peeled
- 1 medium white onion, peeled and quartered
- 1 tablespoon freshly ground black pepper
- 4 fresh chiles serranos or 2 chiles jalapeños, finely chopped
- 1/3 cup white wine vinegar
- 3/4 cup olive oil

FOR THE MEAT
- 12 beef filets (filet mignon), 4 ounces each
- 9 tablespoons olive oil
- 3 tablespoons butter
- Salt to taste
- Black pepper to taste
- 3/4 cup white wine
- 1 cup reduced beef stock

FOR THE SAUCE
- 1/3 cup olive oil
- 1 cup butter
- 1 1/2 medium white onions, peeled and minced
- 8 large garlic cloves, peeled and minced
- 3 1/3 pounds fresh morels or other mushrooms, washed and drained
- Salt and pepper to taste
- 12 ounces creamy Gruyère or semisoft cheese
- 10 ounces Port Salut or mild cheese, cubed

- 1 1/2 cups heavy cream
- 1 1/2 cups sour cream or crème fraîche
- 1 1/3 cups olive oil
- 2 tablespoons butter
- 3 fresh chiles serranos or 2 chiles jalapeños, minced
- 2 bay leaves
- 2 sprigs fresh thyme
- 3/4 cup white wine
- 1/2 teaspoon powdered chicken bouillon or salt to taste

FOR THE GARNISH
- 1/3 cup olive oil
- 1/2 cup butter
- 14 green onions, sliced thinly, or chiles de agua, fresh Anaheim, or banana peppers, washed, seeded, and deveined, sliced lengthwise into narrow slivers
- 6 chiles caribe, Anaheim, or banana peppers, prepared as above
- Salt and pepper
- 1/3 cup olive oil
- 1/3 cup butter
- 24 large squash blossoms, washed and dried
- Salt and pepper
- 2 zucchini, cooked until tender in salted water, drained and sliced thinly

Prepare the marinade: Purée the garlic and onion in a blender or food processor; transfer to a medium glass bowl. Add remaining ingredients and stir well. Pour over the meat and allow to marinate in refrigerator overnight.

Prepare the sauce: Heat a large skillet. Add oil and butter, then add onion and garlic and sauté. Add mushrooms and sauté until liquid has evaporated. Season to taste with salt. Remove 36 mushrooms and set aside for garnishing. Transfer the remainder of the sautéed mixture to a food processor. Add the cheeses and creams, and blend until smooth. Heat a large, heavy saucepan. Add oil and butter. Add, chiles, bay leaves, and thyme, and sauté. Add white wine and reduce to half over medium heat. Add the puréed mushroom mixture to the saucepan. Cook 35 minutes over low heat until sauce has thickened. Season with salt or powdered bouillon. Thin with broth if necessary.

Prepare the garnish: Heat a wok or a heavy skillet with deep sides. Add oil and butter. Add onion and very quickly stir-fry. Add chiles and stir-fry briefly until slightly wilted. Season to taste with salt and pepper and transfer to a bowl; set aside. Reheat the wok or skillet and add oil and butter. Add the squash blossoms to the hot wok and very quickly stir-fry. Season with salt and pepper and set aside. Keep onion garnish and squash blossom garnish warm, or rewarm before using.

Prepare the meat: Remove meat from marinade and drain. Preheat a heavy skillet. Add approximately 3 tablespoons oil and 1 tablespoon butter and heat thoroughly. Add 4 filets to the skillet. Cook 3 to 4 minutes, then turn with tongs and cook another 3 to 4 minutes. Transfer filets to a warm platter. Sprinkle with salt and pepper to taste. Reheat skillet, add the same amounts of oil and butter, and cook 4 more filets. Repeat with remaining 4 filets. (Adding a small amount of meat to the skillet allows it to retain its heat, thus searing the meat so that its juices are retained.)

When all 12 filets are cooked, set them aside. Add wine to pan drippings and reduce to a syrupy liquid. Add beef stock and cook 10 minutes. Transfer the resulting sauce to the large saucepan containing the mushroom-cheese-cream sauce that you prepared earlier. Heat through and season to taste.

To serve: Place a spoonful of sauce on each plate, top with a filet, and garnish with reserved mushrooms, stir-fried onions, chiles, zucchini, and squash blossoms.

SERVES 12

FILETE AL COMINO

Cumin Steak

FOR THE MEAT

    4 chiles guajillos, deveined
    4 chiles anchos, deveined
    4 chiles de árbol
    6 cloves garlic, peeled
    1 onion, quartered
1 1/2 teaspoons cumin
    4 whole cloves
  1/2 cinnamon stick
1 1/2 cups soy sauce
    1 tablespoon freshly ground pepper
3 1/2 pounds filet of beef, such as sirloin
  1/3 cup extra-virgin olive oil
     Aluminum foil
2 1/2 cups chicken broth, reduced to 1 1/2 cups

FOR THE GARNISH

  1/2 cup extra-virgin olive oil
  3/4 cup butter
    6 cloves garlic, finely chopped
  32 small potatoes
     Salt to taste
    1 tablespoon coarsely ground black pepper
    4 medium red onions, thinly sliced crosswise
     Soy sauce to taste
     Salt and pepper to taste
    6 medium zucchini, sliced crosswise into wheels
3 1/2 pounds fresh spinach, washed thoroughly in cold
     water and stems removed
    6 onion slices

Prepare the meat: Preheat a comal or skillet and roast the chiles, garlic, onion, cumin, cloves, and cinnamon, being careful not to burn them. Once they are roasted, blend them with the soy sauce and ground pepper. Make small incisions in the filet and baste it with this marinade.

  Preheat a cast-iron casserole or fry pan, without grease, for 30 minutes. Drain meat and cook, basting occasionally with a bit of oil and turning every 15 minutes to ensure even cooking. The total cooking time is 25 to 30 minutes. Sprinkle with the oil and marinade. Remove the meat from the heat; drain the meat and wrap it loosely in aluminum foil to retain the juices. Set aside. In the same casserole, combine the juices from the meat with the marinade and reduced broth. Simmer for a few minutes until slightly thickened.

  For the garnish: In another casserole, heat 1/3 cup oil with a bit of butter. Add the garlic and cook until golden. Add the potatoes and cover. When they are half done, season them with salt and shake the casserole to ensure even cooking. Sprinkle with the coarsely ground pepper. Preheat a large skillet or frying pan and heat another small amount of oil and butter. Add the red onions and sprinkle with a bit of soy sauce, salt, and pepper. Cook until crispy. Follow the same procedure for the zucchini. Line a large frying pan with a layer of spinach and the onion slices. Season with salt and sprinkle with the rest of the oil and butter. On top of this, place the rest of the spinach and cook until tender.

  To serve: Slice meat thinly and transfer to a warm platter. Garnish with the potatoes, red onions, zucchini, and spinach. Serve the sauce on the side.

SERVES 8

OPPOSITE

A mildly hot spice that, some say, resembles caraway in flavor, cumin is combined here with three types of chile.

The combination of ripe, sweet fruits and pickled chiles adds a pleasing accent to tender slices of pork.

LOMA DE PUERCO EN SALSA DE GUAYABA Y CIRUELA

Pork Loin in Guava and Plum Sauce

Known in Spain as solomillo, *pork loin was adapted for Mexican cuisine and is prepared in a variety of ways. The flavor of this meat is enhanced when it is combined with sweet-and-sour sauces, especially those made with seasonal fruits such as guava and plum.*

FOR THE SAUCE
- 6 large, ripe plums, halved and pitted
- 8 guavas, halved and pitted
- 6 crab apples, peeled and cored
- 1 onion, chopped
- 4 cloves garlic, peeled
- 4 Embassa chiles chipotles in vinegar, deveined
- 1/3 cup vinegar from the chiles
- 4 cloves
- 4 Tabasco peppercorns
- 2 1/2 cups reduced chicken broth
- 6 tablespoons butter
- Salt and sugar to taste

FOR THE PORK
- 2 cups water

- 3 cones *piloncillo* (unrefined brown sugar), or 3 cups brown sugar
- 8 pieces pork loin, 5 to 7 ounces each
- 1/3 cup olive oil
- 1/2 cup butter
- Salt to taste

FOR THE GARNISH
- 4 large purple plums, sliced thinly
- 16 crab apples, peeled, cored, and lightly fried in butter
- 4 ripe guavas, cut into thin strips or chopped, lightly fried in butter
- 8 Embassa chiles chipotles in vinegar

Prepare the sauce: Chop the fruit. In a blender, purée the onion, garlic, chiles, vinegar, cloves, pepper and half the chicken broth. Preheat a saucepan for 5 minutes. Meanwhile, strain the sauce. Add the butter and then add half the strained sauce. (The rest of the sauce will be added at serving time, so that it has a fresh flavor.) Simmer over medium heat for 15 minutes, or until it thickens slightly. Season with a bit of salt and sugar.

Prepare the meat: Preheat the oven to 400°F for 1 hour and preheat a large frying pan for 20 minutes. Bring the water to a boil in a saucepan. Add the brown sugar, and cook over low heat until syrup thickens slightly. Baste the pork loin with this mixture.

In the hot saucepan, put the oil and half of the butter. Brown 4 pork pieces on all sides until a thin, fairly

dark crust forms. Transfer them to an ovenproof baking dish and salt lightly. Repeat procedure with the rest of the meat. Once it is all in the dish, bake it for 10 to 15 minutes. (This baking must be at high temperature in order to keep the meat sealed and juicy.) Remove from the oven and let stand for a few minutes before serving. Cover with aluminum foil to keep warm.

To serve: Warm 6 large plates. Slice the meat thinly and place in the center. On one side of the meat, place the plums; on the other, the crab apples and chiles chipotles. Below, place the guavas. Reheat the sauce and add to it some of that which was left uncooked, along with a bit of broth, so that it is medium thick. Spoon some of the sauce over the meat and serve immediately with remaining sauce on the side.

SERVES 8

MANCHAMANTEL (Stain the Tablecloth)

Meat and Fruit Stew

Some stews, as is the case with this sweet, fruity mole, make your mouth water.

FOR THE MEAT
 20 cups water
 2 onions, quartered
 10 carrots, peeled
 2 heads garlic, separated into cloves
 15 sprigs marjoram
 15 sprigs thyme
  Salt to taste
 3½ pounds pork loin
 6 chicken breasts, cut into quarters

FOR THE STEW
 14 ounces chiles anchos
 8 ounces pine nuts
 10 cloves garlic, peeled
 2½ pounds ripe tomatoes, sliced
 8 cloves

 2 small cinnamon sticks
 1 teaspoon freshly grated nutmeg
 20 sprigs thyme
 10 sprigs marjoram
 1 tablespoon dried oregano, crumbled
 ½ cup butter or oil
 3 cloves garlic, peeled
 1 onion, sliced
  Salt to taste
 10 to 12 cups broth
  Brown or white sugar to taste
 2½ yellow or purple sweet potatoes, sliced, cooked
   in salted water
 6 thick slices pineapple, cut into pieces
 5 ripe, male plantains, sliced in their peels

Prepare the meat: Bring the water to boil in a kettle. Add the onions, carrots, garlic, herbs, and salt. Return to a boil and simmer for 20 minutes. Add the pork loin and simmer gently for 1 hour, or until soft. Add the chicken breasts and cook for 15 minutes. Remove pan from the heat and allow the meat to cool in the broth until lukewarm. Slice the meat thinly and, if you wish, bone the chicken breasts. Reserve the broth.

Prepare the stew: Remove the veins of the chiles and wash. Soak chiles in hot water for 25 minutes. In a blender, purée the chiles, pine nuts, garlic, tomatoes, cloves, cinnamon, nutmeg, thyme, marjoram, and oregano. Strain. Preheat a casserole for 20 minutes. In it, brown the garlic and onions in the butter or oil; remove them and discard. Pour in the chile mixture a little at a time. Season with salt and cook until it changes color and thickens. Add the 10 to 12 cups broth gradually to obtain a slightly thick sauce. Season again and add the sugar, sliced pork, and chicken breasts. Simmer slowly for 20 minutes. Add the sweet potatoes, pineapple, and plantain. Simmer for another 10 minutes. Adjust the seasonings.

To serve: Serve piping hot from the casserole, accompanied by freshly made tortillas.

SERVES 20

OPPOSITE
*A creative selection of spices, combined with potatoes, pineapple,
and plantains, gives this hearty stew a tropical touch.*

Chicken with Almond Mole

The custom of baptism has numerous charms: the infant's dress, the invitations, the church ceremony,
and naturally, the pleasures of the dinner offered in celebration. Traditional dishes are often served,
among them Almendrado, one of the seven classic moles of Oaxaca.
Almonds symbolize the essence of life, so they are perfect in a baptismal dish.

FOR THE CHICKEN
- 10 cups water
- 2 medium white onions, peeled and quartered
- 2 garlic heads, roasted and peeled
- 1 cinnamon stick, 4 inches long
- 8 whole cloves
- Salt to taste
- 2 chickens cut in pieces, or 4 whole chicken breasts or 8 split chicken breasts, approximately 4 1/4 pounds total

FOR THE SAUCE
- 1 1/4 cups lard or vegetable oil
- 1 1/2 medium white onions, peeled and quartered
- 8 garlic cloves, peeled
- 2 cups almonds, blanched

- 1 cup roasted, unsalted peanuts
- 1 cinnamon stick, 4 inches long
- 4 whole cloves
- 16 black peppercorns
- 1 croissant, torn in pieces
- 4 large, ripe tomatoes, roasted
- 8 dried chiles anchos or dried red California chiles, washed, very lightly roasted, seeded, and deveined and soaked in hot water
- 2 slices white onion

FOR THE GARNISH
- 1 can chiles largos or chiles jalapeños, pickled, about 8 ounces (optional)
- 3/4 cup finely chopped blanched almonds or peanuts,
- 2 tablespoons finely chopped fresh parsley

Prepare the chicken: Bring the water to a boil in a large saucepan. Add the onion, garlic, cinnamon, cloves, salt, and chicken. Simmer for 25 minutes or until the chicken is partially cooked. Allow it to cool in the broth. Then remove chicken from the broth and reserve both chicken and broth. Strain the broth.

Prepare the sauce: Heat 3/4 cup lard in a large saucepan. Add the onions, garlic, almonds, peanuts, cinnamon, cloves, peppercorns, and croissant. Cook for 25 minutes. If the mixture begins to stick, add a little more oil or lard. Place the mixture in a blender or food processor. Add tomatoes and chiles, and purée the mix-ture. Heat the remaining 1/2 cup lard in a saucepan. Brown the onion slices. Stir in the puréed mixture and cook until it releases its fat and you can see the bottom of the pan when the mixture is stirred. Add 2 to 3 cups of reserved chicken broth, or as much as is necessary to slightly thin the sauce. Add the chicken and cook for an additional 25 minutes. Correct the seasoning.

To serve: Serve the almond mole from a large clay pot, garnished with canned chiles, chopped almonds or peanuts, and chopped parsley. Accompany with freshly made corn tortillas.

SERVES 20

For a light alternative presentation, use poached chicken, boned, and sliced thinly.
Measure out 2^1/$_2$ cups mole and thin with 1^1/$_2$ cups chicken broth. Serve a fan of sliced chicken breast
over a ladleful of sauce on each individual plate. Garnish with almonds, yellow chiles,
and parsley. Extra mole can be frozen for later use.

Chicken is often the basic ingredient of many traditional recipes.

MOLE POBLANO

Mole (from the City of Puebla)

*"Dearest little Pascual, my Saint Pascual,
I'll offer you this little stew, and you add the seasoning."*

The cuisine of the convent once again inspired Sister Andrea of the Ascension of the Convent of Santa Rosa to create this mole *(stew), based on a pre-Columbian sauce. In it, the good Sister combined chiles, herbs, and spices. The dish was served in honor of Viceroy Count de Paredes and Marquis of Laguna, and to the Bishop Don Manuel Fernández de Santa Cruz, who authorized the tiling of the convent kitchen with rustic Talavera porcelain as thanks for the fine food that came out of it.*

FOR THE SPICES
3 cups butter
2^1/$_2$ onions, chopped
8 cloves garlic, peeled
^{3}/$_4$ cup sesame seeds
^{3}/$_4$ cup almonds
^{3}/$_4$ cup peanuts
^{3}/$_4$ cup raisins
1 cup pitted prunes
1^1/$_2$ ripe, male plantain, peeled
1 teaspoon coriander
^{1}/$_2$ teaspoon anise
2 cinnamon sticks
1 butter horn or croissant, torn in pieces
1 onion, peeled
1 head garlic
3 large tomatoes
10 tomatillos
2 tortillas
6 cups chicken broth, hot
2 slices onion
Salt to taste

FOR THE CHILES
30 chiles mulatos, slit lengthwise and deveined

16 chiles anchos, slit lengthwise and deveined
16 long chiles pasillas, slit lengthwise and deveined
3 chiles chipotles, slit lengthwise and deveined
1^1/$_2$ onions, chopped
6 cloves garlic, peeled
Salt to taste
^{1}/$_2$ pound baker's chocolate in 4 pieces
4 tablespoons sugar
8 to 10 cups chicken broth

FOR THE CHICKEN
20 cups water
6 thighs
12 breasts, halved (or 24 roasted, boned Cornish hens)
2 large onions, quartered
1 head garlic, separated into cloves
3 carrots, peeled
^{1}/$_2$ celery stalk, chopped
6 bay leaves
Salt to taste

FOR THE GARNISH
^{1}/$_2$ cup sesame seeds, toasted

Prepare the spices: Heat a little of the butter in a deep stew pot. Fry the onions until transparent and lightly golden. Remove onions and reserve them. Fry the garlic the same way, until golden brown, and reserve. Add a little more butter to the pot and fry the sesame seeds, almonds, and peanuts; remove and reserve them. Add 2 tablespoons butter to the pot and fry the raisins, prunes, plantain, coriander, anise, cinnamon, and butter horn. On a comal or hot skillet, roast the onion, garlic, tomatoes, and tomatillos. Scorch the tortillas over an open flame. Purée the fried and roasted ingredients together with the chicken broth in a processor, metate, or grinder twice. Cook the onion slices in the remaining butter until golden brown. Add the blended mixture and season. Cook the stew over low heat for 1 1/2 hours or until it forms a paste. Stir occasionally with a wooden spoon so that it doesn't stick.

Prepare the chiles: On a preheated skillet, lightly roast the chiles. Be careful not to roast them too much, or they will become bitter. Wash and soak the chiles in salted water (the amount of time depends on how spicy you want the stew to be—about 1 1/2 hours). Blend the chiles well, along with the onion, garlic cloves, and a bit of the water in which the chiles were soaked. Strain this mixture and pour it in increments into the spice mixture in the stew pot. Allow 10 minutes between each addition. Cook the stew on low heat, stirring occasionally. Season with salt. Add the chocolate and sugar. Continue cooking for 3 or 4 more hours. Lightly cover the stew pot with aluminum foil, so that it doesn't spatter. (In days gone by, the stew was cooked in patio ovens or wood fireplaces, which gave it a distinct flavor.) The stew's sauce will be thick and oily. Pour in chicken broth to thin it as needed, re-seasoning each time.

Prepare the chicken: Heat the water in a pot. Add the thighs and breasts. Add the onions, garlic, carrots, celery, bay leaves, and salt, and simmer for 20 minutes. Set aside to cool. Add the chicken to the stew and cook another 30 minutes. Strain broth and reserve for another use.

To serve: Serve the stew in a casserole and sprinkle it with toasted sesame seeds. Or serve the chicken pieces on individual plates. Cover them with the sauce and sprinkle with toasted sesame seeds. Serve with red rice, stewed beans, and freshly made tortillas.

SERVES 24

VARIATION

Pepare the stew with hens marinated in salt, pepper, butter, and a bit of garlic for 1 hour
in the bottom of the refrigerator. Bake them in a preheated oven at a high temperature for 40 minutes
or until golden brown. Cool, split the breasts, and arrange them on the thighs.

NOTE

Always make more sauce than needed, since stew can be poured over fried or poached eggs.
You can also make enmoladas (stew-filled pies with flaky crusts) or crêpes filled with
chicken, cheese, and cream. Another simple way to serve it is over red rice.
The sauce freezes well in hermetically sealed containers.

Mole Poblano is generally served on special occasions, such as baptisms, weddings, and birthday parties. Its preparation is believed to be overseen by Saint Pascual Bailón, the patron saint of cooking.

Stuffed Cornish Hens in Orange Sauce

When my mother traveled to Monterrey to visit my Aunt and Uncle Fernández every year,
she used to look forward to this succulent dish, made with the large, sweet, seedless oranges grown in the area.
The recipe hints at the Sephardic Jewish influence that is present in Monterrey regional cooking.

FOR THE CORNISH HENS
   6 Cornish hens, about 1/2 pound each
   6 garlic cloves, peeled and puréed
1 1/2 medium white onions, peeled and grated
   1 tablespoon freshly ground black pepper
   1 tablespoon ground cinnamon
   1/2 teaspoon ground cloves
1 1/2 tablespoons powdered bouillon or salt
1 1/2 cups orange juice
1 1/2 cups tangerine juice
   1/3 cup olive oil
   3 cups cooked rice, prepared with almonds,
      raisins, and pine nuts
   1/3 cup butter, cut into small pieces
   1/2 cup butter, at room temperature

FOR THE SAUCE
   4 tablespoons butter
   1 medium white onion, peeled and grated

   1 teaspoon freshly grated black pepper
   1 cinnamon stick, about 4 inches long
   6 whole cloves
   6 whole allspice
   3 bay leaves
   6 cups orange juice
   2 cup tangerine juice
   2 cups chicken broth, reduced to 2/3 cup
   1 cup *piloncillo* or brown sugar
      Salt to taste
1 1/2 to 2 tablespoons cornstarch, dissolved in 1/2 cup
      water or broth
   8 tablespoons butter

FOR THE GARNISH
   4 orange peels, fruit removed and peels cut into "baskets"
   4 oranges, peeled and sectioned
   1/2 cup almonds, blanched and sliced on the diagonal
   2 bunches spearmint

Prepare the Cornish hens: Place the hens in a large glass bowl. Add garlic, onion, pepper, cinnamon, cloves, bouillion, orange juice, tangerine juice, and olive oil. Marinate a minimum of 4 hours at room temperature, or in the refrigerator. Toss rice with 1/3 cup butter. Stuff the hens with prepared rice.

Preheat oven to 450°F. Butter a baking dish. Place the hens in the baking dish and spoon remaining marinade over them. Dot hens with butter and bake for about 1/2 hour, then lower heat to 350°F and continue baking hens, basting occasionally, for another 1/2 hour or until crispy. When hens are done, remove from oven and cover with aluminum foil; set aside for about

20 minutes. Remove and save the pan drippings.

Prepare the sauce: Place pan drippings in a saucepan. Add 4 tablespoons butter, onion, pepper, cinnamon stick, cloves, allspice, bay leaves, orange and tangerine juices, chicken broth, piloncillo, and salt. Stir well, then simmer until reduced by half. Add the dissolved cornstarch and simmer sauce until it thickens and becomes translucent, about 20 minutes. Stir in 8 tablespoons butter. Keep the sauce hot.

To serve: Arrange the hens on a large serving platter. Baste with sauce. Serve rice on the side. Garnish with orange baskets, filled with orange sections and decorated with almonds and spearmint sprigs.

SERVES 12

Squab, Jalisco Style

Hunting is popular in Jalisco, where squab and quail are abundant.

FOR THE SAUCE

1/2 cup olive oil

16 chiles anchos, seeded, deveined, washed, and
dried

1 quart water

1/3 cup red-wine vinegar

6 cloves garlic, peeled

1 medium white onion

1 teaspoon oregano, dried and crushed

1 teaspoon ground cumin

1 teaspoon black peppercorns

Salt to taste

FOR THE SQUAB

8 squab or quail, 3 to 3 1/2 ounces each, cleaned
and singed

1/2 cup olive oil

8 teaspoons butter, in pieces, plus 1/2 cup butter

Dried oregano to taste

FOR THE GARNISH

8 masa casseroles

8 sprigs parsley

Prepare the sauce: Heat oil in a frying pan. Add chiles and sauté just until wilted. Remove. Mix water and vinegar. Soak chiles in this mixture for 40 minutes. Remove chiles, and reserve soaking water.

In a blender or food processor, purée chiles with garlic, onion, oregano, cumin, peppercorns, salt, and a little soaking water.

Prepare the squab: Put squab in a baking dish, and top with sauce. Drizzle with a little of the oil, dot with butter pieces, and sprinkle with oregano; let stand for 1 hour.

Remove birds from sauce; reserve sauce. Preheat a heavy skillet for 25 minutes. Heat remaining olive oil and 1/2 cup butter. Fry squab for 8 to 10 minutes or until done, turning and basting continually with sauce. Remove birds from pan.

Simmer sauce for a few minutes, until thick. Halve squab.

To serve: Place a masa casserole on each of 8 plates. Cover with sauce. Top with 2 squab halves, pour sauce over squab, and garnish with parsley.

Roasted squab is served with
an individual masa casserole.

PATO A LA VERACRUZANA

Duck, Veracruz Style

Duck has been part of Mexican cuisine since before the Conquest. In this dish,
the duck has a creamy texture and the traditional flavors of Veracruz.

FOR THE DUCK
- 2 large ducks, 5 pounds each
- 14 cups water
- 1/2 bunch celery, sliced
- 1/2 leek, sliced
- 3 cups white wine
- 2 medium onions
- 10 whole cloves
- 10 black peppercorns
- Salt to taste

FOR THE SAUCE
- 8 chiles anchos, slit lengthwise, and deveined
- 3/4 pound almonds, skinned
- 5 cloves garlic, peeled
- 2 teaspoons cumin
- 4 whole cloves
- 3 egg yolks
- 28 ounces Del Fuerte seasoned, puréed tomatoes
- 4 tablespoons corn oil
- Salt to taste
- 2 to 3 cups duck broth, skimmed
- 7 1/2 ounces canned Embassa chiles jalapeños in oil and vinegar marinade
- 1 cup stuffed olives
- 1/2 cup capers

FOR THE GARNISH
- 4 cups cooked white rice
- 1/2 cup olives
- 1/3 cup capers
- 4 ounces Embassa green chile strips
- 7 1/2 ounces Embassa red pepper strips
- Sprigs of cilantro, washed

Prepare the duck: Wash the ducks in boiling water. Burn the tails with alcohol. Pluck the ducks and wash them again. Soak them in hot water to soften the fat, and cut them into pieces. In a saucepan, heat the water with the celery, leek, wine, onions, cloves, peppercorns and salt. When it comes to a boil, add the ducks. Cook for 1 1/2 hours or until tender, being careful not to overcook. Leave them to cool in the liquid, then refrigerate and skim the fat from the broth. Save the broth for the sauce.

Prepare the sauce: Roast the veinless ancho chiles on a preheated comal or skillet. Wash them and soak them in a bit of water for 1/2 hour. In a blender, combine the almonds, garlic, spices, egg yolks and puréed tomatoes. In a saucepan heat the oil and add the mixture. Cook over low heat for 25 minutes or until it thickens, stirring constantly with a wooden spoon. Season to taste and pour in the heated, skimmed duck broth. Add the ducks and cook over low heat for some minutes more. Add the jalapeño strips along with half their liquid, the olives, and the capers. Continue cooking slowly for 20 more minutes and adjust the seasoning. The sauce should be medium thick.

To serve: Form rice into mound shape and arrange duck around it. Baste with the sauce and garnish with the rest of the olives, capers, green chile strips, red pepper strips, and cilantro sprigs.

SERVES 8

OPPOSITE
Braising (a slow, gentle method of cooking) is what makes this duck exceptionally tender.

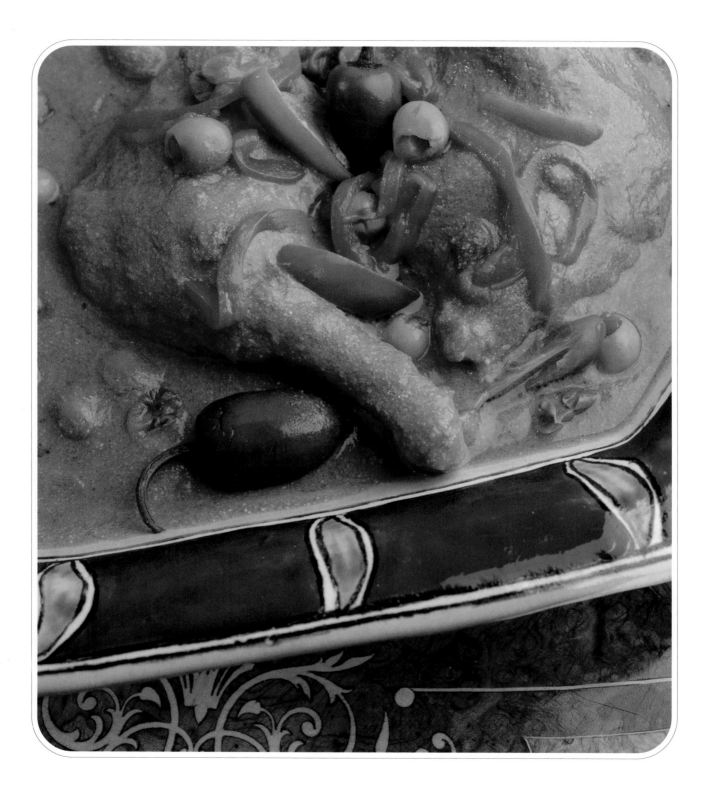

AMARILLO DE SAN MATEO DEL MAR

Yellow Seafood Mole, San Mateo Del Mar Style

The Isthmus of Tehuantepec is inhabited by Zapotecs, Mixes, and Huaves. The Ikoods, a special group of Huaves, fish the tranquil lagoons of San Mateo del Mar rather than the rough ocean. The waters of the open sea are so powerful, they inspire respect and fear. The Ikoods ask for the protection of the gods in special rituals, feasts, and dances dedicated to the turtle, the serpent, the storm, and the sea. The importance of fishing always stands out in these rituals. During the windy season, they eat many dishes with shrimp and fish, called escamas. *Amarillo, an intense yellow sauce, is one of the preferred* moles *of the people who live near the coast.*

FOR THE FISH AND SHRIMP MOLE
- 3 large ripe plum tomatoes
- 1 1/2 medium white onions, peeled
- 6 large cloves garlic, peeled
- 10 dried chilcosle chiles or 8 dried chiles anchos, seeded and deveined
- 6 dried chiles guajillos or New Mexico chiles, seeded and deveined
- 10 ripe tomatillos, husked and boiled
- 14 black peppercorns
- 1/2 cinnamon stick
- 1 tablespoon achiote (annatto) seeds, ground
- 4 whole cloves
- 1/2 teaspoon cumin seeds
- 3/4 cup vegetable oil or lard
- Salt to taste
- 1/2 cup fresh masa (corn dough)
- 6 cups fish stock
- 2 1/2 pounds salted striped mullet, or any dried fish, cut into 2-inch squares and soaked in water to cover for 1 day with 2 changes of water
- 1 1/2 pounds shrimp, peeled, and deveined
- 4 to 6 fresh hoja santa leaves or 10 fresh avocado leaves

FOR THE DUMPLINGS
- 1 pound fresh masa
- 1/3 cup water
- 1/2 tablespoon lard or bacon drippings
- Salt to taste
- 1/2 cup chopped cilantro or epazote

FOR THE GARNISH
- 2 medium white onions, peeled and finely chopped
- 1 cup finely chopped radishes
- Fresh lemon juice to taste
- Salt to taste

Prepare the mole: Preheat a comal or a heavy skillet and roast the tomatoes on all sides, turning them often. Roast the onions, garlic, and chiles. Soak the roasted chiles briefly in water. Drain the chiles and place in a blender or a food processor with the tomatoes, onions, garlic, tomatillos, and spices, and purée.

Heat the oil in a large saucepan. Add the puréed chile mixture and stir-fry until the oil separates from the sauce. Season with salt. Dissolve the masa in a little of the fish stock and stir the mixture into the sauce. Remove the fish from the soaking liquid and pat dry. When the sauce thickens, add the fish, shrimp, and hoja santa leaves to the sauce. Simmer uncovered for another 20 minutes over medium heat.

Prepare the dumplings: While the sauce is simmering, place the masa in a large bowl. Add the water a little at a time and then the lard, salt, and cilantro. Work the dough until smooth. Using about 1 1/2 teaspoons of dough for each, form small balls or dumplings. Use your fingers to make an indentation on one side of each ball. Add the dumplings to the sauce along with enough of remaining stock to make a light but not soupy consistency.

To serve: Spoon the mole onto a serving platter and serve with the chopped onions and radishes on the side. Sprinkle with lemon juice and salt. Accompany with freshly made tortillas.

SERVES 8

Most people think of mole as a hearty dish containing meat. Here, however, is a lighter yet equally satisfying version of this traditional dish which contains seafood.

LANGOSTA EN SALSA DE TAMARINDO DE LA COSTA OAXAQUEÑA

Oaxacan Lobster in Tamarind Sauce

The Oaxacan coast is one of outstanding beauty and its Puerto Escondido is spectacular.
Its name, which loosely translates as "hidden port," comes from fishermen who wanted to keep this
beautiful location a secret. Rock oysters, mother-of-pearl oysters, manta rays that jump out of the water, and
enormous lobsters with a very delicate flavor all can be found in the waters near the shore.

FOR THE SAUCE
- 1/2 cup butter
- 1/2 cup olive oil
- 2 medium onion, peeled, and chopped
- 6 medium cloves garlic, peeled, and chopped
- 2 1/2 cups puréed fresh pineapple
- 1 cup fresh apricot jam
- 2 1/2 cups tamarind pulp (available in Asian or Latin markets), or 3 pounds fresh tamarind, soaked, cleaned, and puréed
- 1 cinnamon stick (about 2 inches long)
- 6 whole cloves, ground
- 1 cup brown sugar or grated *piloncillo* (unrefined brown sugar), or to taste
- 1/2 cup cider vinegar
  Salt to taste
- 1 to 2 cups chicken stock

FOR THE LOBSTER
- 1/2 cup clarified butter
- 1/2 cup olive oil
- 3 heads garlic, peeled
- 2 cups water
- 1/4 cup cider vinegar
- 6 dried chiles guajillos, anchos, or New Mexico chiles, lightly toasted in a warm skillet
- 12 dried chiles japonés or costeños, lightly toasted in a warm skillet
- 4 dried chiles de árbol, lightly toasted in a warm skillet
- 4 whole cloves, ground
- 1/2 teaspoon black peppercorns
- 1/2 teaspoon cumin seeds
  Salt to taste
- 8 lobster tails, shells removed, deveined, and rinsed
- 1/3 cup olive oil

FOR THE GARNISH
- 1/3 cup olive oil
- 24 dried chiles de árbol
- 8 fresh pineapple slices (each about 1 inch thick)
- 8 ears corn, cooked in water with a little salt and sugar
- 4 cups white baby beans, cooked in water with onion and garlic
  Fresh oregano leaves

Prepare the sauce: Heat a wok or a large casserole and add the butter and the oil. When the butter is melted, add the onions and cook until they are caramelized. Add the garlic and continue cooking for about 10 minutes more. Add the remaining ingredients, except the chicken stock, and cook uncovered over low heat until the sauce starts to reduce and becomes thick, about 40 minutes. Stir in small amounts of the chicken stock until the sauce has a creamy consistency. Continue cooking uncovered for about 20 more minutes. Remove the cinnamon stick, adjust the seasoning, and set aside.

Prepare the lobster: Purée the butter, olive oil, garlic, water, and vinegar in a blender or a food processor. Add the chiles, spices, and salt, and purée. Put the lobster tails in a shallow dish and pour the marinade over them. Let stand 30 minutes to 1 hour. (The lobster tails can be covered and refrigerated overnight, if desired.) Preheat a large skillet and add the olive oil. Transfer the lobster tails from the marinade to the skillet and cook, covered, for 4 to 6 minutes. Do not overcook the lobster tails; they should remain moist and tender. Season with salt.

Prepare the garnish: Preheat a medium casserole. Add the oil and stir-fry the chiles. Set aside. Prepare the remainder of the garnish.

To serve: Warm 8 large soup plates. Spoon the warmed tamarind sauce onto the bottom of each plate. Place a lobster tail on top and garnish the sides of the plate with the stir-fried chiles, a pineapple slice, an ear of corn, and the white beans. Sprinkle with oregano and serve immediately.

SERVES 8

NOTE
Cooked lobster tails can be sliced and served on top of a small pool of tamarind sauce.

BOMBA DE PESCADO

Fish Bombe

*This recipe was created by the author for the first Mexican Cooking Festival, held
in December 1984 in Acapulco. Most of Mexico's top chefs cooked for that event,
which was attended by prominent food editors from the United States.*

FOR THE STUFFING
- 1/2 cup vinegar
- 1/2 cup olive oil
- 3 cloves garlic, puréed
- Salt to taste
- 1 teaspoon freshly ground pepper
- 8 chiles anchos, seeded, deveined, and lightly roasted

FOR THE FISH
- 8 red snapper, grouper, or flounder fillets, 6 to 8 ounces each
- 2 tablespoons finely chopped garlic
- 1 tablespoon freshly ground pepper
- Salt to taste

FOR THE SAUCE
- 1 quart fish stock
- 4 chiles anchos, lightly roasted, seeded, deveined, and soaked in water for 20 minutes
- 1 medium white onion, coarsely chopped
- 4 cloves garlic, peeled
- 5 1/3 tablespoons butter
- Salt to taste
- 1 quart crème fraîche
- 2 cups half-and-half
- 1 1/2 tablespoons corn starch, dissolved in 1 cup water
- 1 cup freshly grated Parmesan cheese

FOR THE DOUGH
- 2 1/2 pounds puff-pastry dough, cold

FOR THE GLAZE
- 2 egg yolks
- 1 egg
- 2 tablespoons half-and-half

Prepare the stuffing: Combine vinegar, oil, garlic, salt, and pepper in a glass bowl. Add chiles and macerate for 2 hours.

Prepare the fish: Put fillets in a baking dish large enough to hold them in a single layer. Do not stack. Sprinkle with garlic, pepper, and salt. Fold over to enclose seasonings. Cover and refrigerate for 1 hour.

Prepare the sauce: Reduce fish stock to 1 1/2 cups. Blend chiles in a blender or food processor with onion and garlic. Heat butter in a frying pan. Add chile mixture and fry until thick. Season with salt. Add reduced fish stock, crème fraîche, half-and-half, dissolved corn starch, and salt, and simmer for 25 minutes or until sauce thickens slightly. If it becomes too thick, add a little more half-and-half. Stir in cheese. Keep warm.

Preheat oven to 375°F. Grease 3 baking sheets, and wet lightly.

Prepare the dough: On a floured surface, roll out dough into a 1/8-inch-thick sheet. Cut eight, 3 1/2- to 4-inch circles and eight, 4- to 4 1/2-inch circles.

Place small circles on baking sheets. Spread with chile stuffing, and top with fish. Cover with large circles, and press circles together to seal edges.

Beat egg yolks with egg and half-and-half. Brush top of bombes with egg mixture to glaze. Bake for 40 minutes or until golden brown. Remove from oven.

To serve: Spoon sauce to cover a platter. Arrange fish bombes on sauce. Pass extra sauce in a bowl.

SERVES 8

*Mexican fish dishes
may be intricate
preparations, such as
Fish Bombe,
which was created
for a cooking festival.*

Filet of Sole with Chile Mulato and Baby Eel

In this recipe, the flavor of the fish is enhanced by steaming.

6 tablespoons butter
6 tablespoons extra-virgin olive oil
2 medium purple onions, finely chopped
4 chiles mulatos, cut in thin strips
  Salt and pepper to taste

4 strips of parchment paper, cut in half
8 sheets aluminum foil
8 sole filets, 5 to 6 ounces each
2 small cans baby eels

Preheat oven to 400°F. In a pan heat butter with oil and fry onions until soft and translucent. Add the chile strips and season. Set aside.

Soak the parchment until soft; drain. Line each foil sheet with a parchment strip and top with a sole filet. Cover with sauce, a spoonful of fried onion, and 1 tablespoon of baby eel, with a little of its oil. Fold the parchment over the fish and cover tightly with the foil paper so the filets are totally enclosed. Bake for 8 to 12 minutes. Serve hot.

SERVES 8

Sole is a very delicate flatfish, highly appreciated for its white meat.
One side of its body is flat and light in color, while the side on which both its eyes are located, is dull,
grayish, and rounded. It also bears a characteristic black stain on its chest fin.

ALMEJAS CHOCOLATES

Chocolate Clams

This species of clam is gathered near the seashore, kept in mesh cages, and delivered live to the marketplace.

48 chocolate clams or any small, fresh clams, in
    shells

16 limes, halved
Tabasco sauce

Clean clams in sea water or fresh water. Open them, and rinse again. Detach each clam from the shell, and remove the stomach by making two incisions. Place clam in shell, and fold over the orange fringe of the clam.

To serve: Divide clams among 8 plates. Squeeze fresh lime juice and sprinkle Tabasco sauce over clams to taste.

SERVES 8

*Fresh chocolate clams—which have nothing to do with chocolate but are simply known by this name—
are eaten with a squirt of lime juice and a dash of Tabasco sauce.*

GRANOS Y VERDURAS
◆
GRAINS AND VEGETABLES

ARROZ A LA MEXICANA

Mexican Rice

This rice can be prepared with black bean broth instead of water, and adding 1 chile mulato.
Serve it with roasted chiles poblanos stuffed with clams and beans or with sopecitos and salsas.

FOR THE RICE
   3 cups long-grain white rice
1 1/2 cups corn oil
   3 cloves garlic, peeled
   1 onion, quartered

FOR THE SAUCE
  28 ounces Del Fuerte seasoned, puréed tomatoes

   3 cloves garlic, roasted
1/2 onion, roasted
3 1/2 cups water
   2 tablespoons powdered bouillon, or to taste
   3 fresh chiles *cuaresmeños*
   8 sprigs parsley

Prepare the rice: Soak the rice in a bowl of hot water for 15 minutes. Rinse with cold water until the rice water runs clear. Drain. In a saucepan, heat the oil and lightly brown the garlic and onion. Add the rice, stirring occasionally until golden brown. Drain off the oil.

   Prepare the sauce: In a processor, blend the puréed tomatoes with the roasted garlic and onion. Add the mixture to the rice and fry for a few minutes,

or until it changes color. Add the water, season, and add the chiles cuaresmeños. Cover tightly and cook over low heat for 40 minutes, shaking the saucepan occasionally so that the rice doesn't stick together and the grains look whole. Remove the garlic and onion pieces. Leave the chiles as a garnish.

   To serve: Transfer the rice to a warm platter, and serve with freshly made tortillas and red and green salsa.

SERVES 8

OPPOSITE
Mexican rice is a colorful dish that invites thousands of interpretations.

BUDÍN DE ARROZ CON RAJAS DE CHILE POBLANO

Rice and Chile Casserole

This soufflé-like casserole is exquisite. My mother learned to prepare it
from my grandmother. It is a good dish for a brunch buffet.

FOR THE SAUCE
- 1/2 cup corn oil
- 7 garlic cloves, peeled
- 2 large white onions, peeled and sliced diagonally
- 12 chiles poblanos, roasted, sweated, and peeled; seeded and deveined; soaked in salted water for 20 minutes to remove piquancy; cut into strips
- 6 large ripe tomatoes
- 1 medium white onion, peeled and quartered
- Salt to taste
- Black pepper to taste

FOR THE CREAM
- 2 cups crème fraîche or 1 cup heavy whipping cream whisked with 1 cup sour cream

- 2 cups plain yogurt
- 1/2 teaspoon salt
- 1/2 teaspoon freshly ground black pepper
- 2 cloves garlic, peeled and pressed
- 2 1/2 cups fresh mozzarella, Oaxaca, or string cheese
- 2 cups creamy Monterey Jack, Gruyère or Chihuahua cheese

FOR THE TOPPING
- 5 egg whites
- 1/4 teaspoon salt
- 4 egg yolks, beaten lightly

FOR THE RICE
- 5 to 6 cups cooked white rice

Prepare the sauce: Heat the oil in a medium saucepan. Brown 4 garlic cloves, then remove and discard. Sauté the onion slices in the same oil until transparent. Stir in chile strips and cook for another 5 minutes. In a blender or food processor, grind the tomatoes with the raw onion and remaining 3 cloves garlic. Strain the tomato mixture and stir in the sautéed onion and chile strips. Season to taste with salt and pepper, and continue cooking over low heat for another 30 minutes or until the sauce thickens.

Prepare the cream and cheese: Stir together the cream and the yogurt. Season with salt, pepper, and garlic. Set aside. Grate cheeses and set aside.

Prepare the topping: Beat egg whites with salt until stiff. Then carefully fold in egg yolks.

To assemble the casserole: Preheat oven to 350°F. Butter a deep baking dish. Spoon half the rice into the dish and cover with half the tomato-chile sauce. Then place a layer of half the cream on top. Sprinkle half the grated cheese over dish. Repeat a second layer of rice, using remainder of rice. Repeat layers of sauce, cream, and grated cheese until all the ingredients are incorporated. Spread the prepared topping over the casserole and bake for 45 minutes or until the topping is golden brown. Serve immediately.

SERVES 8 TO 12

OPPOSITE
A rich, elegant side dish that will enliven any main course.

FRIJOLES BORRACHOS

Drunken Beans

Drunken beans are a representative dish of the area around Monterrey, one of the first regions to enjoy beer.

FOR THE BEANS
1 1/2 pounds dried pinto beans, cleaned, rinsed, and
    soaked overnight in water to cover
3 to 3 1/2 quarts water
1 large white onion, halved
6 cloves garlic, peeled
1 tablespoon lard or vegetable oil

FOR THE SAUCE
1/2 cup lard
1 large white onion, finely chopped
3 large tomatoes, finely chopped
4 chiles serranos or chiles jalapeños, finely
    chopped
1 1/2 to 2 cups finely chopped cilantro
    Salt to taste
2 cups light or dark beer

Prepare the beans: Put beans in a pressure cooker. and add enought water to cover. Add onion, garlic, and lard; cover and cook for about 45 minutes to 1 hour. If preparing in a regular pot, put the beans in a deep casserole, and add 3 times their volume in water. Add onion, garlic, and lard. Cook over low heat for 1 1/2 to 2 hours or until beans are tender. If water evaporates, add more warm water.

Meanwhile, prepare the sauce: Heat lard in a heavy frying pan. Add onion, and fry until lightly browned. Add tomatoes, chiles, and cilantro. Add the cooked beans, salt to taste, and beer. Adjust seasoning, and continue to cook over low heat until mixture thickens, about 45 minutes.

To serve: Pour hot beans into a clay or ceramic serving dish. Serve with roasted kid or other meat and corn or flour tortillas.

SERVES 8

TORTA DE ELOTE

Corn Torte

This is a perfect dish to prepare ahead of time for a baptismal party. Corn, called "Our Mother" and "She Who Sustains Us" in many Indian languages, is so central to the sustenance of life in Mexico and throughout the Americas that a corn dish seems fitting to welcome a new soul.

3/4 cup butter
1 cup sugar
7 to 8 cups kernels from ripe ears of corn
1/4 cup whipping cream
1/4 cup milk

5 eggs, separated
2 tablespoons flour
3 tablespoons rice flour
1 tablespoon baking powder
1 teaspoon salt

Preheat oven to 350°F. Butter a round 9-inch cake pan or bundt pan, line with waxed paper, then butter the waxed paper and sprinkle with flour.

Beat the butter until creamy, about 10 minutes. Add the sugar and beat another 8 minutes. Place the corn kernels, cream, and milk in a blender or food processor and purée. Beat the egg yolks. Add corn purée to the butter-sugar mixture, alternating with egg yolks. Then sift together the flour, rice flour, baking powder, and salt and add to the mixture. Beat the egg whites until they form soft peaks and fold gently into the mixture. Spoon into prepared pan and bake in preheated oven for about 35 to 45 minutes or until golden brown.

SERVES 8 TO 12

NOTE

Pre-Hispanic Mexican agriculture was based on the sacred triad of corn, beans, and squash. When Europeans arrived, they referred to Indian *mais* by the word they used for the staple grain of any country, a word that also meant any small granular object: *corn*. The magical corn is actually a grass plant with giant seeds, or kernels.

VERDOLAGA SALTEADA CON RAJAS

Stir-fried Purslane with Poblano Chiles

A versatile vegetable known since pre-Hispanic times, purslane can be used raw in salads or stir-fried in cooked dishes.

¹/₄ cup olive oil
2¹/₂ medium white or yellow onions, sliced into thin wedges
6 chiles poblanos, roasted, sweated in a clean, wet dishcloth for 5 minutes, peeled, deveined, and sliced into thin strips (*rajas*)
3 pounds fresh purslane (you may substitute watercress), rinsed well, patted dry, and stems removed, leaving at least 3 inches on top
Salt to taste

Prepare the purslane: Preheat a large wok or heavy frying pan over medium-high heat. Add oil, and heat through. Add onion, and stir-fry, until the onion is transparent yet crisp. Add the *rajas* and the purslane, and stir-fry, tossing the vegetables continuously. Continue cooking for a few minutes until *al dente*. Season to taste.

To serve: Divide the stir-fried purslane among 8 deep soup bowls and serve with freshly made tortillas and salsas.

SERVES 8

POSTRES ◆ DESSERTS

SOMBRERO DE CHOCOLATE

Chocolate Hat

Chocolate is native to Mexico. Before the Conquest, Indians used cocoa beans in hot drinks,
enjoying chocolate for its natural bitter taste or sweetening it with locally produced honey.

FOR THE CHOCOLATE HAT
Parchment paper
1 1/2 pounds bittersweet chocolate, in pieces
7 ounces sweet chocolate, in pieces
17 ounces milk chocolate, in pieces

FOR THE SAUCE
9 Manila mangoes, peeled, pitted, and sliced
1 1/2 cups sugar
1/3 cup Kahlúa or other coffee liqueur

1/4 cup tequila
1 teaspoon lime juice
3 cups fresh orange or tangerine juice

FOR THE GARNISH
1 quart lime sherbet
1 quart fig sherbet
1 quart blackberry sherbet
6 bougainvillea branches or other flower branches
(optional)

Prepare the chocolate hat: From parchment paper, cut a circle 15 inches in diameter (for base of the hat), a circle 8 inches in diameter (for top of the hat), and a rectangle 5 X 15 inches.

Bring water to a boil in a double boiler from which steam does not escape. Melt bittersweet, sweet, and 11 ounces milk chocolate together, stirring occasionally. When chocolate reaches 85°F on a candy thermometer, remove from heat.

Pour half the chocolate onto a marble or metal surface. Keep remaining half warm in the double boiler. Cool chocolate on marble surface by stirring constantly with a spatula until it reaches 75°F. Add remaining chocolate, and mix well. With a spatula, spread enough chocolate to cover the 15-inch circle with a 1/4-inch-thick layer of chocolate. Repeat with the 8-inch circle. Set aside for 3 hours to cool or until hard. Keep remaining chocolate warm in double boiler. Do not overheat.

Using some of the remaining melted chocolate, recoat both circles with a 1/8-inch-thick layer, reserving enough for the parchment rectangle. Curl up the sides of the large circle to form the hat's brim.

Form the parchment rectangle into a cylinder, stapling to keep its shape. Spread this cylinder with the last of the melted chocolate. Cool slightly, and brush to give texture. Place upright on baking sheet, and cool. Peel off paper.

Peel paper from large circle, and place chocolate on a 16-inch round plate.

Melt remaining 6 ounces milk chocolate. Cover large circle with a thin layer of melted milk chocolate, and center the cylinder upright on top. Cover cylinder with a little melted chocolate. Peel paper from small circle, and place on top of cylinder.

Prepare the sauce: Purée all ingredients in a blender or food processor. Strain.

To serve: Decorate brim of hat with scoops of sherbets and bougainvillaea branches. (You may substitute other fresh-fruit sherbets.) Serve with mango sauce on the side.

SERVES 24

OPPOSITE
Chocolate Hat is decorated with scoops of fresh-fruit sherbet, bougainvillaea blossoms, and strawberries.

SORBETE DE MANGO

Mango Sherbet

Mango sherbet can be made from fresh or canned fruit. Fresh mangoes are plentiful from March to September.

FOR THE SYRUP
2½ cups sugar
2 cups plus 1 tablespoon water

FOR THE SHERBET
3½ pounds mango pulp

Ice cubes
Coarse salt (kosher salt)

FOR THE GARNISH
24 strawberries
8 mint leaves

Prepare the syrup: Combine sugar and water in a medium saucepan. Bring to a boil over high heat. Stir with a wooden spoon, making sure sugar is well dissolved. Stop stirring. Bring mixture to a rolling boil. Remove from heat, and immediately pour into a bowl. Cool.

Prepare the sherbet: The day before serving, purée mango in a blender or food processor, and pour into a glass bowl. Add cooled syrup, stir, and let stand for 10 minutes. Grind ice, and mix with salt. Place in a large bowl. Set mangoes in bowl on the ice to chill thoroughly. Beat mixture by hand or pour into an electric ice cream maker. Process until sherbet sets. Freeze overnight.

To serve: Mound sherbet balls one on top of another. Garnish with strawberries and mint leaves.

MAKES 2 QUARTS

SORBETE DE HIGO

Fig Sherbet

FOR THE SYRUP
2½ cups sugar
2 cups plus 1 tablespoon water

FOR THE SHERBET
3½ pounds fresh figs, peeled

Ice cubes
Coarse salt (kosher salt)

FOR THE GARNISH (OPTIONAL)
½ watermelon shell, sliced llengthwise
16 figs, halved

Prepare the syrup: Put sugar and water in a medium saucepan. Bring to a boil over high heat. Stir with a wooden spoon, making sure sugar is well dissolved. Stop stirring. Bring mixture to a rolling boil. Remove from heat, and immediately pour into a bowl. Cool.

Prepare the sherbet: The day before serving, purée figs in a blender or food processor, and pour into a glass bowl. Add cooled syrup, stir, and let stand for 10 minutes. Grind ice, and mix with salt. Place in a large bowl. Set figs in bowl on the ice to chill thoroughly. Beat mixture by hand or pour into an electric ice cream maker. Process until sherbet sets. Freeze overnight.

To serve: Fill watermelon shell with scoops of sherbet, and garnish with figs.

MAKES 2 QUARTS

CHURROS

Long Fritters

*Churros are a typical Mexican sweet snack that originated in colonial times,
when they were so savored with a cup of piping hot chocolate or coffee and milk.*

1 quart water
1 1/2 to 2 teaspoons salt
3 cups flour
1 teaspoon baking powder

4 egg yolks
3 cups vegetable oil or corn oil
2 limes, halves
Sugar to taste

Mix water and salt in a saucepan. Bring to a rolling boil. Remove from heat. Combine flour and baking powder, and add to water all at once. Stir to form smooth dough. Return to heat, and cook, stirring, until smooth. Remove from heat, and stir in egg yolks, one at a time. Continue to beat until the dough becomes smooth and elastic. Cool.

In a frying pan, heat oil and limes. Test with a bit of dough. When oil spatters, it is hot enough. Put dough in a churro mold or a pastry bag fitted with a star-shaped tip. Press out 4- to 4 1/2-inch strips. Fry in oil until brown on all sides, turning to cook evenly. Drain on paper towels. Then roll in sugar.

To serve: Place hot churros on a tray.

MAKES ABOUT 25 CHURROS

OVERLEAF, CLOCKWISE FROM LEFT
*Fritters, Michoacán bread, pastries, earthenware mug
filled with* piloncillo *(unrefined brown sugar) syrup to be
poured over Fritters, chocolate rounds of Morelian Hot
Chocolate, sugar-coated Long Fiitters, Curds in Syrup in
green dish, and guava paste.*

BUÑUELOS

Fritters

Buñelos are a traditional Mexican dessert, often served around Christmas.
Maria Dolores Torres Yzabal, a Mexico City caterer, shared this recipe for a delicious dessert.

FOR THE FRITTERS
  1 tablespoon dry yeast
  $1/2$ cup warm milk
  6 cups flour
  1 teaspoon salt
  8 egg yolks, beaten until thick
  4 egg whites, beaten until soft peaks form
  2 tablespoons sugar
  2 tablespoons butter, softened
  1 teaspoon anise

  $2^1/_3$ cups lard or corn or saflower oil
  $1/2$ to 1 cup boiling water, containing 10 tomatillo
    husks
  2 quarts vegetable oil

FOR THE SYRUP
  6 cones *piloncillo* (unrefined brown sugar), or 6
    cups dark brown sugar
  4 sticks cinnamon, each 4 inches long
  6 guavas, thinly sliced

Prepare the fritters: Dissolve yeast in milk. Put flour, salt, egg yolks, egg whites, and yeast mixture in a bowl. In an aluminum bowl, mix sugar, butter, anise, and $1/3$ cup lard. Add flour mixture, and knead with hands, adding a little boiling water, to form dough. Continue kneading dough on a floured pastry board until glossy, elastic and not sticky. Form a ball, and grease with a little lard. Cover, and set dough aside until doubled in volume.

  Heat oil and 2 cups lard in a deep frying pan. Divide dough into 20 balls. Turn a clay pot upside down. Cover bottom with a dish towel. Sprinkle towel with flour. Roll out 1 dough ball on a floured surface to a circle 3 to 4 inches in diameter. Place on the floured dish towel, and carefully stretch circle until it measures $8^1/2$ to 9 inches in diameter. The dough will be very thin and almost transparent.

  Fry in hot oil, 3 to 4 minutes, turning once. When crisp, remove fritter from oil, and drain on a paper towel. Repeat procedure for remaining 19 dough balls.

  Prepare the syrup: In a medium saucepan, heat sugar, water to cover, cinnamon, and guava. Cook over high heat for 45 minutes to 1 hour or until a thick syrup is formed.

  To serve: Break buñelos into quarters, and place 4 quarters in each individual shallow bowl. Cover with hot syrup.

MAKES 20 BUÑELOS

FLAN

Caramelized Egg Custard

*This classical dessert is a regional specialty throughout Mexico, appearing in many characteristic guises.
In some areas it is flavored with coconut, in others with cheese or squash.*

2¹/₂ cups sugar
1¹/₃ cups water
10 eggs plus 4 egg yolks
2 cups sweetened condensed milk

2 cups whole milk
2¹/₂ cups evaporated milk
2 tablespoons vanilla extract

Prepare the burnt sugar topping: Combine the sugar and water in a heavy saucepan. Stir well, then simmer over low heat until the sugar totally dissolves and the mixture is dark brown.

Pour the burnt sugar into a 10-inch ungreased ring mold, tipping the mold to evenly line the bottom. Set aside to cool.

Preheat the oven to 350°F.

Prepare the custard: Beat the egg and egg yolks. Place the three milks in a separate mixing bowl and stir well. Blend eggs and milk, then stir in the vanilla. Pour custard into the prepared ring mold. Place in a larger mold or pan filled with 1 inch of water. Bake for 1¹/₂ hours or until a toothpick inserted into the center comes out clean. Allow to cool, then refrigerate overnight.

Unmold before serving. Serve chilled.

SERVES 8 TO 12

POSTRE DEL VIRREINATO

Viceroy's Cake

FOR THE BATTER
12 eggs, separated
3/4 cup sugar
4 1/2 ounces potato starch or corn starch, sifted twice
4 1/2 ounces (generous 1 cup) flour, sifted
1/2 teaspoon baking powder

FOR THE CUSTARD
1 cup water
3 1/3 cups sugar
16 egg yolks
1 tablespoon ground cinnamon
1/2 cup sweet sherry, or to taste

FOR THE FILLING
1/2 cup chopped figs
1/2 cup chopped orange

1/2 cup chopped candied citron
1/3 cup chopped lime
1 cup dry sherry

FOR THE FROSTING
4 egg whites
2 1/2 cups heavy cream, chilled in freezer for 1 hour
1 cup powdered sugar

FOR THE GARNISH
1/2 cup sweet sherry, approximately
3 figs, sliced in strips
1 orange, sliced in strips
2 limes, sliced in strips
12 almonds, toasted
1/4 cup pink or blond pine nuts

Preheat the oven to 350°F. Grease and flour 2 8-inch round cake pans.

Prepare the batter: Beat egg yolks with an electric mixer until thick. Gradually add sugar. Continue beating until very thick and sugar is completely dissolved. Combine potato starch, flour, and baking powder. Gradually add to egg-yolk mixture. Set aside.

Beat egg whites in large bowl until stiff. Carefully fold into egg-yolk mixture. Fill cake pans equally with batter. Bake for 30 minutes or until cake springs back when gently pressed with fingertip. Cool for 10 minutes in pans. Invert on cake racks. Cool cakes.

Prepare the custard: Heat water and sugar in a heavy saucepan, stirring until sugar dissolves. Boil without stirring until syrup forms a hard ball (260°F on a candy thermometer). Remove from heat. Cool slightly. Beat egg yolks in a bowl until creamy, and slowly add syrup, beating until mixture thickens a little. Add cinna-mon. In a double boiler, cook custard over simmering water, stirring constantly, for 20 to 30 minutes, until thick and creamy. Remove from heat, and stir in sher-ry. Cool. Refrigerate for several hours.

Prepare the filling: Put figs, orange, citron, and lime in a glass bowl, and macerate in sherry for 1 hour.

Prepare the frosting: Beat egg whites until stiff. In another bowl, beat chilled heavy cream until it thickens. Add sugar, and beat until soft peaks form. Carefully fold in egg whites, and refrigerate until serving time.

To assemble cake: Place a layer of cake on a but-tered cake plate, and sprinkle with about 1/4 cup sher-ry. Cover with a layer of custard. Layer macerated fruit over custard. Top with second cake layer. Sprinkle with sherry. Repeat custard and fruit layers. Frost top and sides with frosting, and garnish with figs, oranges, limes, almonds, and pine nuts.

Refrigerate cake for 2 hours before serving.

SERVES 8 TO 12

Desserts served during the colonial period were rich and usually liqueur-based. Several of these desserts were the creations of convent kitchens to please royalty.

BEBIDAS ◆ DRINKS

INDEX